ARCHAEOLOGY OF AKBAR'S 'IBADAT-KHANAH AT FATEHPUR SIKRI 1576-1582 A.D.

D. V. SHARMA

ARCHAEOLOGY OF AKBAR'S 'IBADAT-KHANAH AT FATEHPUR SIKRI

(1576 - 1582 A.D.)

D. V. SHARMA

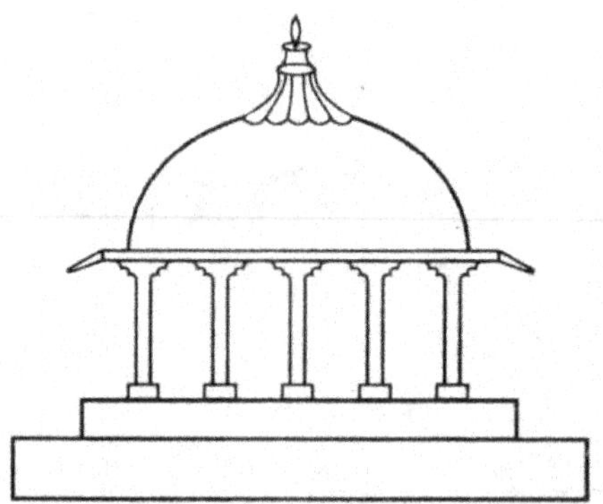

The Historical Research Documentation Programme

AGRA

ALL SUBJECT TO AGRA JURISDICTION

Published by
The Historical Research Documentation Programme

The Heritage

Art & Architecture Book Shop,
G-14, Akhilesh Tower,
Hariparvat, M.G. Road,
AGRA - 282 002
(INDIA)
Telephone : (0562) 2153524

Figures (Drawings) by
Shahid Zaman Khan of National Graphics, Agra

Archaeology of
Akbar's 'Ibādat-Khānah at Fatehpur Sikri

Published by Ajay Nath for the Historical Research Documentation Programme, Agra. Laser Type setting by Yogesh Agrawal

TO

THE PEOPLE OF HINDUSTAN

whom Akbar emancipated

from

Theocracy and State Tyranny

and

instituted

THE 'IBADAT-KHANAH AT FATEHPUR SIKRI

to give the message of

SULḤ-I-KUL

(Universal Peace)

BIBLIOGRAPHICAL ABBREVIATIONS

AN-III   : **Akbar-Namah** of Abū'l Faẓl, Vol. III (tr. by H. Beveridge) (Delhi, 1973)

Arif   : **Tārīkh-i-Akbarī** (or **Tārīkh-i-Qandahārī**) of Muhammad Arif Qandahārī (tr. by Tasneem Ahmed) (New Delhi)

B & L   : **Fatehpur Sikri : A Source Book** by Michael Brand and G.D. Lowry (Cambridge, U.S.A. 1985)

CAMA   : **Calligraphic Art in Mughal Architecture** by R. Nath (Calcutta, 1979)

Correia-Afonso : **Letters from the Mughal Court**, by John Correia-Afonso (Bombay 1980)

FPS-1972   : **Fatehpur Sikri** by S.A.A.Rizvi (A.S.I. New Delhi, 1972)

FPS MONU   : **Fatehpur Sikri and Its Monuments** by R. Nath (Agra, 2000)

FTC   : **Architecture of Fatehpur Sikri** : Forms, Techniques and Concepts, by R. Nath (Jaipur, 1988)

Gaur   : **Excavations at Fatehpur Sikri** by R.C. Gaur (New Delhi, 2000)

HMA-II   : **History of Mughal Architecture** by R. Nath, Vol. II : Akbar (1556-1605 A.D.) (The Age of Personality Architecture) (New Delhi, 1985)

Indica, 39-1	:	'On the Identification of Akbar's **'Ibādat-Khānah** at Fatehpur Sikri' by R. Nath, *Indica* Bombay, Vol. 39 No.1 (March 2002) 51-60
Marg	:	**Fatehpur Sikri**, ed. by M.Brand & G.D.Lowry (Marg Bombay 1987)
Monserrate	:	**'Commentarius'** of Father Anthony Monserrate, tr. from Latin into English by J.S. Hoyland (London, 1922)
MT-II	:	**Muntakhabu't-Tawārīkh** of Badaoni, Vol.II (tr. by W.H. Lowe) (Delhi, 1973)
Rizvi	:	**Fatehpur Sikri** by S.A.A. Rizvi and V.J.A. Flynn (Bombay, 1975)
TA-II	:	**Ṭabaqāt-i-Akbarī** of Nizamuddin Aḥmed, Vol. II (tr. by B. De) (Calcutta, 1936)

LIST OF ILLUSTRATIONS

Figures

Plates

The *'Ibādat-Khānah* (1576-82 A.D.) which Akbar founded at Fatehpur Sikri for religious and philosophical discussions was one of his greatest and the most famous institutions. It culminated in the establishment of the *Dīn-i-Ilāhī* (1582) and the doctrine of *Sulḥ-i-Kul* (Peace to all, Universal Peace). But, inspite of the historians' and archaeologists' consistent efforts for more than a century, its actual site had not been traced and its was a hot controversy. Like the problem of the decipherment of the Indus Valley script, the scholars have been claiming, of and on, to have solved this riddle and to have discovered it. These claims, based on pre-conceived notions as they were, rather than on honest interpretation of ground realities of history and archaeology, could not be sustained and collapsed. How to co-relate its description of the contemporary Persian historians with the archaeological evidence in-situ - was the basic problem which they missed. At such a site as Fatehpur Sikri where construction went on for nearly a decade, one has always to be aware of the chronological sequence of architecture, to be able to notice the overlapping of structures, in order to identify the different phases of construction with the help of archaeology. One who has no acquaintance with the Persian sources, and no understanding of the archaeological evidence in-situ, or of the Personality of Akbar, or of the spirit of Fatehpur Sikri, is liable to commit blunders like the one which has been done recently (in 2002) when a false claim of its identification has been made and an altogether NEW historical building has been created in the name of 'Conservation'.

With these tools and by this methodology, we have traced, identified and established the *'Ibādat-Khānah* with fair amount of certainty. We have discussed its Institution, Situation and Composition, respectively, in the first three chapters. The fourth chapter is exclusively devoted to the study of Archaeological Remains of the *'Ibadāt-Khānah* and the fifth to the Archaeological Analysis of the Recent Claims of its Identification which is a sort of *Ṭikā* (Commentery) to set the record straight. Full references have been given. Drawings (17) and Plates (57) have been used to illustrate the points of study. Thus have we tried to make up the best possible documentation of this subject.

Since I joined the Agra Circle of the Archaeological Survey of India in 1998, as Superintending Archaeologist, I have been studying the monuments of Fatehpur Sikri archaeologically, in the field. This monograph on *'Ibādat-Khānah* is, in fact, part of my Ph.D. thesis entitled : *'Archaeology of Fatehpur Sikri'* prepared under the guidance of my Guru Professor R. Nath, M.A., Ph.D., D.Litt. (Retired Professor & Head of the Department of History and Indian Culture, University of Rajasthan, Jaipur) who is one of most renowned scholars of the subject. His fifty years' experience of field-work at Agra and Fatehpur Sikri, his numerous papers, articles, lectures and most importantly his three books :

1. **History of Mughal Architecture**, Vol. II (New Delhi 1985)

2. **Architecture of Fatehpur Sikri** (Concepts, Norms and Techniques) (Jaipur 1988), and

3. **Fatehpur Sikri and Its Monuments** (Agra 2000)

have been greatly useful in the preparation of this work. Truly, this monograph, on such a controversial subject as this, could not have been raised without these solid foundations. The Guru's debt is irrepayable and I will not play truant by just paying formal thanks to him.

I thank Shri R. B. Sharma, proprietor of the Joshi Resort, Fatehpur Sikri Road, Kiraoli (Agra), his sons and staff, for extending all help and cooperation during our stay there when this work was written. I also thank Shri Shahid Zaman Khan of National Graphics Agra for drawings and computer work, and Shri Ajay Nath (proprietor of the HRD Programme Agra) for publishing this work in a nice format.

I am also thankful to my mother and wife, and my children Bharat, Abhimanyu and Vandana & Mr. Vinod Kumar, ASI Photographer for his photographs.

- D. V. Sharma

Agra : 27 October 2002

CONTENTS

CHAPTERS

Chapter-1

The Institution of the 'Ibādat - Khānah

Jalāluddīn Muhammad Akbar, son of Humayan and grandson of Babur, was born and brought up in sheer adversity. His early fourteen year's life, from his birth in A.H. 949/1542 A.D. at Umarkot when his father was fleeing for life, to his accession to the throne in 963/1556 at Kalanaur, is full of **hardship, suffering and struggle**. It was, in fact, on this solid bedrock that his personality was made up. A man of iron-will and firm determination; courage and enthusiasm; lion's fearlessness; dare-devil initiative and discretion; inexhaustible resourcefulness; indefatigable energy, perseverance and dedication; and a wonderful common-sense- **he was a genius flower** which blossomed in the difficult conditions of a medieval life.[1]

Akbar inherited a small kingdom. Of it, he made and left behind a vast **Empire,** a firmly established **state** with its own political and administrative institutions and, above all, a **court-culture** which set the ideal way of life in the country. All this was his own doing. Soon after his accession in 1556 A.D., **he realized that theocratic polity was the weakness of the Muslim state in India.** It had completely alienated the people and, like an exotic phenomenon, it was struggling for bare survival. To plant this state, root-and branch, into the soil and the land over which he aspired to rule, it was necessary to emancipate it from its **Arabic complexion**, and to make it an essentially **Indian thing.**[2]

With this objective in view, he initiated a series of bold **innovations**, e.g. abolition of the hated '*Jaziyā*' (poll tax upon the Hindus) and other discriminatory taxes; matrimonial alliance with the native Rajput kingdoms; proceedings of the '*Ibādat - Khānah* **(The House of Religious Discourses)** (1576); institution of the *mansabdārī* (constitution of nobility according to military ranks awarded on merit by the Mughal state) and *Mahzar* (the Sacred Decree of the King) (1579); promulgation of the *Dīn–i–Ilāhī* (the Religion of God) (1582); and the *Tarīkh-i-Ilāhī* (the Solar Calendar of God) (1584); and adoption of such Indian customs as the **Sun-worship** and the *Jharokhā-Darshan* (1572-85); and *Rākhī, Tilaka (Tīkā,* formal recognition of the Rajput rulers of vassal states) and *Tulā–Dān* (annual solar and lunar weighing of the King), which changed its form and fabric, and **revolutionized the whole Indian scene.**[3] It is remarkable that all these measures were adopted by him at Fatehpur Sikri during the period from 1572 to 1585 A.D.

These innovations were intended to repudiate **Theocracy** which the '*Ulema* had been trying to impose upon the Sultanate in the name of the religion of Islam, and to suppress **Pan-Arabism** which that orthodoxy sought to establish. He reverred the cultural institutions of the people and adopted them, not only as personal rituals, but also as the natural behaviour of his state, in imitation of the *Cakravartīn* sovereigns of the country.[4] *Jharokhā – Darshan*, for example, became an **essential and indispensable daily ritual of the Mughal Emperor**, from Akbar to Shah Jehan.

Akbar liberally patronised Indian literatures in Sanskrit, Persian and Hindi; and native Fine Arts as Music, Painting and Architecture under regular departments called '*kārkhānahs*' (lit. workshops). With firm and bold deliberation, he proceeded to establish cultural rapport and rapprochement with the people so that the Mughals could live and grow in India, as had lived and grown the Guptas and the Pratiharas.[5] This policy of Akbar was based on the doctrine which is generally called '*Sulh-i-Kul*' (Peace to all).

Akbar's contemporary historian Badāonī has recorded in his Persian work: the *Muntakhabu'l-Tawārīkh*, that in A.H. 982/1575 A.D. Akbar commissioned a building "consisting of four halls, near the new palace in Fathpur."[6] This is confirmed by other historians, Abu'l Fazl[7] and Nizamuddin.[8] It was completed in the following year 983/1576 and named '*Ibādat – Khānah*.[9] Badaoni noted that the **purpose of its institution was to hold philosophical discourses and to settle religious controversies.**[10] This is also confirmed by Abu'l Fazl[11] and Nizāmuddin.[12] Badāonī specifically mentioned, in this respect, that he (Akbar) **held meeting** "in this building. Shaikhs, '*Ulema* and pious men and a few of his own companions and attendants were the only people who were invited. **Discussions** were carried on upon all kinds of instructive and useful topics."[13] This shows that it was not a temple or mosque, but a **place for conference for holding disussions on religious and philosophical querries and controversies**, and no religious worship or rituals were performed there, as it is sometimes misunderstood owing to its literal meaning being a 'House of '*Ibādat* or Worship.'[14]

Badaoni has discussed the *raison-d'etre* of the '*Ibādat – Khānah* elaborately. Thus he recorded:

> "The cause was this. For many years previously the Emperor had gained in succession remarkable and decisive victories. The empire had grown in extent from day to day; everything turned out well, and no opponent was left in the whole world. His Majesty had thus leisure to come into nearer contact with ascetics and the disciples of his reverence (the late) Muin (Shaikh Muin-ud-din Chisti Sigizi of Ajmer) and passed much of his time in discussing the word of God (the Quran) and the word of the Prophet (Hadith). Questions of Sufism, scientific discussions, enquiries into Philosophy and Law, were the order of the day. His Majesty spent whole nights in praising God; he continually occupied himself in pronouncing *yā huwa* (O God) and *yā hādi* (O Guide) in which he was well-versed. His heart was full of reverence for Him, who is the

true Giver, and from a feeling of thankfulness for his past successes he would sit many a morning alone in prayer and meditation on a large flat stone of an old building which lay near the palace in a lonely spot, with his head bent over his chest, gathering the bliss of the early hours of dawn. When then he heard that Sulaimān Kararānī, governor of Bengal, used every night to offer up the prayers in the company of some 150 persons consisting of renowned Shaikhs and Ulemā,' and used to remain in their society till morning listening to commentaries and exhortations, and then, after offering up the morning prayers, would occupy himself in state-business, and the affairs of the army, and of his subjects: and that he had his appointed time for everything and never broke through his good rule: and when also news arrived from Badakhshan of the coming of Mirzā Sulaimān, who was a prince of Sufi tendencies, and had become a Sāhib-i-hāl, (one who attains the state of ecstasy and close union with God) and a Murīd: for these urgent reasons he had the very cell of Shaikh 'Abdullah Niyāzi Sarhindi (who had formerly been a disciple of Shaikh Islām Chishti, but had afterwards joined the circle of Mahadeva) (Siva) repaired, and built a spacious hall on four sides of it. He also finished the construction of the tank called *Anup Talao*. He named that cell the '**Ibādat - Khānah**.[15]

"On Friday after prayers, he would go from the new chapel (*Jāmi' Masjid*) of the Shaikh'ul-Islam, and hold a meeting in this building. Shaikhs, *Ulema* and pious men, and a few of his own companions and attendants were the only people who were invited.[16] **Discussions** were carried on upon all kinds of instructive and useful topics. One day Jalāl Khān Qurchī, who was my patron and the means of introducing me to court,[17] **in the course of conversation and disputation** made the following statement......He (Akbar) assembled a party in his (Shaikh Ziya-Ullah's) honour at the *Ibādat - Khānah*, and every Thursday evening he invited Sayyids ,Shaikhs, *Ulema* and Amīrs. But ill feeling arose in the company about the seats and order of precedence, so His Majesty ordered that the Amīrs should sit on the east side, the Sayyids on the west, the *Ulemā* on the south, and the Shaikhs on the north.[18] His Majesty would go from time to time to these various parties and **converse with them and discuss philosophical subjects**. Quantities of perfume were used and large sums of money were distributed as rewards of merit and ability among the worthy people who obtained an entry through the favour of the Emperor's courtiers..."[19]

"All at once, one night, the vein of the neck of the *Ulema* of the age swelled up, and a horrid noise and confusion ensued. His Majesty got very angry at their rude behaviour and said to me, 'In future report any of the *Ulema* who talk nonsense and cannot behave themselves, and I shall make him leave the hall.' I said gently to Asaf Khan, 'If I carried out this order, most of the *Ulema* would have to leave' when his Majesty suddenly asked what I had said. On hearing my answer, he was highly pleased and mentioned my remark to those sitting near him."[20]

It appears, by Badaoni's narrative, who constantly participated in the proceedings of the *'Ibādat - Khānah*, that in its first phase when the *'Ibādat - Khānah* was open only for the scholars of Islam, and *'pundits'* of other religions were not admitted into it, it was used for exposing the ignorance and hypocrisy of the orthodox *mullas* and the *maulvis* who were used to run the State by the Canon Law and professed theocracy. Thus Badaoni noted:

> "He used to summon *Makhdūm 'ul-Mulk* Maulana 'Abdullah Sultanpuri to that assembly in order to annoy him; and **would set up to argue against him** Haji Ibrahim, and Shaikh Abu'l-Fazl, then a new arrival, but now the prime leader of the New Religion and Faith or rather the infallible guide and expositor together with several other new-comers. His Majesty **used to interrupt** the Maulānā at every statement with interjections and observations........."[21]

This is confirmed by the letters from Frs Acquaviva, Monserrate and Hanriques to Chief Fathers of the order of St.Paul.Goa, during their stay at the Mughal Court (from 1579 to 1582).[22] Their letter dated 13th July 1580 referred to a **fire-test** which certain Shaikh proposed to be held to prove the supremacy of the *Qurān*. The Fathers noted that the Shaikh "was a **criminal** who deserved death and that he (Akbar) wished him to die in that manner in order not to arouse the people."[23] Precisely he used the *'Ibādat - Khānah*, in the first phase, to suppress the bigoted *Mullas*.[24]

According to Badaoni, Akbar put up several **controversial issues** for discussion before the assemblies in the *'Ibādat - Khānah*, for example, the matter of legal *'nikah'* and *'mut'ah'* marriages was raised and debated at length.[25] The *'Ulema* could not be unanimous on any point and there were conflicting opinions. These **discourses and disputations** on philosophical and religious matters exposed the intellectual weakness of the *'Ulemā*, and soon, Badaoni laments, Akbar lost faith in Islam. Though he (Badaoni) accused Mulla Muhammad of Yazd, Birbal, Abu'l Fazl and Hakim Abu'l Fath, for turning the Emperor from Islam and leading him " to reject inspiration, prophetship, the miracles of the Prophet and of the saints, and even the whole law,"[26] it were chiefly the proceedings of the *'Ibādat Khanah* which shook his faith in Islam and led him to inquire of truth in other quarters.[27]

How the Mullā - Maulvis fought with each other in the *'Ibādat - Khānah* and their narrow-mindedness disappointed the King has been plainly recorded by Badaoni in his narrative of the events of the year 986/1578-79:

> "And later that day the Emperor came to Fathpur. There he used to spend much time in the *'Ibādat - Khānah* in the company of learned men and Shaikhs. And especially on Friday nights, when he would sit up there the whole night continually occupied in discussing questions of Religion, whether fundamental or collateral. The learned men used to draw the sword of the tongue on the battle-field of mutual contradiction and opposition, and the antagonism of the sects reached such a pitch that they would call one another fools and heretics.

The controversies used to pass beyond the differences of Sunni, and Shiah, of Hanifi and Shafi's, of lawyer and divine, and they would attack the very bases of belief. And Mukhdum-ul-Mulk wrote a treatise, to the effect that Shaikh 'Abd-un-nabi had unjustly killed Khizr Khan Sarwani, who had been suspected of blaspheming the Prophet (peace be upon him) and Mir Habsh, who had been suspected of being a Shiah, and saying that it was not right to repeat the prayers after him, because he was undutiful towards his father, and was himself afflicted with hemorrhoids. Shaikh 'Abd-un-nabi replied to him that he was a fool and a heretic. Then the Mullas became divided into two parties, and one party took one side and one the other, and became very Jews and Egyptians for hatred of each other. And persons of novel and whimsical opinions, in accordance with their pernicious ideas, and vain doubts, coming out of ambush decked the false in the garb of the true, and wrong in the dress of right, and cast the Emperor, who was possessed of an excellent disposition, and was an earnest searcher after truth, but very ignorant and a mere tyro, and used to the company of infidels and base persons, into perplexity, till doubt was heaped upon doubt, and he lost all definite aim, and the straight wall of the clear Law, and of firm Religion was broken down, so that after five or six years not a trace of Islam was left in him: and every thing was turned topsy-turvy."[28]

The second phase of the *'Ibadat - Khanah* began when it was opened also to the *'pundits'* of other religions, such as "Sufi, philosopher, orator, jurist, Sunni, Shia, Brahman, Jati (*Yati* or *Jogi*), Siura, (shravaka, Jaina), charbaka (materialists), Nazarene (Roman Catholic Padres), Jew, Sabi (Sabian), Zoroastrian (Parsee) and others" in the words of Abū'l Fazl.[29] Philosophical questions were debated with them. Badaoni noted: -

"Crowds of learned men from all nations, and sages of various religion and sects came to the Court, and were honoured with private conversations. After inquiries and investigations, which were their only business and occupation day and night, they would talk about profound points of science, the subtleties of revelation, the curiosities of history, and the wonders of traditions, subjects of which large volumes could give only an abstract and summary: and in accordance with the saying:- "three thing are dangerous, Avarice satisfied: desire indulged: and a man's being pleased with himself" everything that pleased him, he picked and chose from any one except a Muslim, and anything that was against his disposition and ran counter to his wishes he thought fit to reject and cast aside. From childhood to manhood, and from manhood to his declining years the Emperor had combined in himself various phases from various religions and opposite sectarian beliefs, and by a peculiar acquisitiveness and a talent for selection, by no means common, had made his own all that can be seen and read in books. Thus a faith of a materialistic character became painted on the mirror of his mind and the storehouse of his imagination, and from the general impression this conviction took form, like an engraving upon a stone, that there are wise men to be found and ready at hand in all religions, and men of asceticism, and recipients of revelation and workers of miracles among all nations and that the truth is an inhabitant of every place and that consequently how could it be right to consider it as confined to one religion or creed, and that, one which had only recently made its appearance and had not as yet endured a thousand years! And why assert one thing and deny another, and claim pre-eminence for that which is not essentially pre-eminent ? And Samanas (Buddist ascetics) and Brahmans (who as far as the matter of private interviews is concerned gained the advantage over every one in attaining the honour of interviews with His Majesty, and in associating with him, and were in every way superior in reputation to all learned and trained men for their treatises on morals and on physical and religious sciences, and in religious ecstacies, and stages of spiritual progress and human perfections) brought forward proofs based on reason and traditional testimony, for the truth of their own, and the fallacy of our religion, and inculcated their doctrine with such firmness and assurance, that they affirmed mere imagination as though they were self evident facts, the truth of which the doubts of the sceptic could no more shake -

"Than the mountains crumble, and the heavens be cleft"

And the Resurrection, and Judgement, and other details and traditions, of which the Prophet was the repository, he laid all aside. And he made the courtiers continually listen to those revilings and attacks against our pure and easy, bright and holy faith (viz. Islam)."[30]

Badaoni further recorded that a Brahman named Devi, a Sufi philosopher Shaikh Taju'd-Din and a Shia scholar Mulla Muhammad Yazdi, were pulled up the balcony of the Imperial castle (=Palace) on a *charpai* (cot) and, thus suspended in the air, they instructed the King in the philosophies of Hinduism, Sufism and Shia'ism, respectively.[31] Not only the Roman Catholic Padres were invited from Goa, fire worshippers (Zoroastrians, Parsees) were also invited from Navsari (Gujarat) and appraised Akbar of the religion of Zardust, "and taught him the peculiar terms, the ordinances, the rites and ceremonies of the Kaianians."[32] The Jaina sources overwhelmingly confirm that Jaina *munis (Acharyas)* as Jinachandra Suri, Hiravijaya Suri and Bhanuchandra, regularly visited Akbar and acquainted him with the Jaina religion.[33]

These philosophical discourses at Fatehpur Sikri, held in the *'Ibādat - Khānah* (1576-82) impressed upon Akbar the "futiliy of the orthodox point of view of Islam and he rejected it. Abu'l Fazl, unequivocally, recorded the net result of the proceedings of the *'Ibādat Khānah* **in the words of Akbar himself** as follows:

"Most persons, from intimacy with those who adorn their outside, but are inwardly bad, think that outward semblance, and the letter of Muhammadanism, profit without internal conviction. Hence we by fear and force compelled many believers in the Brahman (i.e. Hindu) religion to adopt the faith of our ancestors. Now that the light of truth has taken possession of our soul, it has become clear that in this distressful place of contrarities (the world), where darkness of comprehension and conceit are heaped up, fold upon fold, a simple step can not be taken without the torch of proof, and that that creed is profitable which is adopted with the approval of wisdom. To repeat the creed, to remove a piece of skin (i.e. to become circumcised) and to place the end of one's bones on the ground (i.e. the head in adoration) from dread of the Sultan, is not seeking after God."[34]

A close study of the proceedings of the *'Ibādat - Khānah*, thus, shows that Akbar used it, in second phase, to suppress **Islamic Orthodoxy**.

His purpose for instituting the *'Ibādat - Khānah*, having thus been fulfilled, assemblies of *'Ibādat - Khānah* were gradually discontinued, and **these were held, instead, in the King's Private apartments** which the court historian Abū'l Fazl has referred to as Private Audience Hall:

> "His Majesty is accustomed to spend the hours of the night profitably; to the *private audience hall* are then admitted eloquent philosophers and virtuous Sufis, who are seated according to their rank and entertain His Majesty with wise discourses. On such occasions His Majesty fathoms them, and tries them on the touch-stone of knowledge or the subject of an ancient institution is disclosed, or new thoughts are hailed with delight. Here young man of talent learn to revere and adore His Majesty, and experience the happiness of having their wishes fulfilled, whilst old man of impartial judgement see themselves on the expense of sorrow, finding that they have to pass through a new course of instructions.

> "There are also present in these assemblies, unprejudiced historians, who do not mutilate history by adding or suppressing facts, and relate the impressive events of ancient times. His Majesty often makes remarks wonderfully shrewd, or starts a fitting subject for conversation. On other occasions matters relating to the empire and the revenue are brought up, when His Majesty gives orders for whatever is to be done in each case. About a watch before daybreak, musicians of all nations are introduced, who recreate the assembly with music and songs, and religious strains; and when four *gharis* are left till morning His Majesty retires to his private apartments, brings his external appearance in harmony with the simplicity of his heart, and launches forth into the ocean of contemplation."[35]

Correia-Afonso, after a close study of the letters of Roman Catholic Padres of the First Jesuit Mission to the Akbar (1579-82), also concluded similarly:

> "After his return from Kabul, Akbar seems to have resumed for a time the theological debates interrupted by the war, **and these were now conducted in the King's private apartment rather** than in the *Ibādat - Khānah*. Attendance at these sessions declined gradually, and by the end of 1582, Akbar's inclination towards the observance of Hindu rites was sufficiently clear."[36]

This was **complete negation of the theocratic character of the State** which cast a religious duty upon the king to devote himself entirely to the cause of Islam and to proclaim *'jihād'* (Holy war) against the non-believing subjects, as Barni propounded in the *Fatwa-i-Jahandari.'* Akbar upheld the basic principle of Islam preached in the *Quran,* II.256. that there cannot be use of force in religious matters and the *Quran,*IX.29 that *'jihad'* be directed only against those who are atheists and do not believe in God, or in the merits and demerits of their deeds which will be judged on the Last Day, and protect (i.e. treat them as *'Zimmis'*) your subjects even if they do not believe if they pay the *'Jaziya'* and let them live their own life in peace.[37]

The proceedings of the *'Ibādat - Khānah* finally led Akbar to establish the *Din-i-Ilahi* and the doctrine of *'Sulh-i-Kul'* (Peace to all). Correia-Afonso, thus, aptly noted:

> "...Sometime in 1582. Akbar called a Council and invited to it all the masters of learning and the military commandants of the Cities round about,...... the Council. with the single exception of Raja Bhagwan Das endorsed **Akbar's plan for the Din-i-Ilahi.** a new religion or society which the eclectic Emperor compounded out of elements from Islam, Hinduism Jainism, and Zoroastrianism. It is hard to find any Christian influence in the *Din-i-Ilahi.*"[38]

The intellectual proceedings of the *'Ibadat - Khanah,* in fact, helped Akbar to adopt a thoroughly **liberal policy** to live in peace with his subjects, as well as his nobles, and led him to put into practice the doctrine of *'Sulh-i-Kul'* (Peace to all). in total negation of *'Pan-Arabism.'*

****

References

1.   Cf. FPSMONU, p.1.
2.   Ibid, pp.1-2.
3.   Ibid, p.2 and Preface p.xi.
4.   Ibid, 2-3.
5.   Ibid, 3.
6.   *MT*, II. 200.
7.   *AN*, III. 157-58.
8.   *TA*, II. 470-71.
9.   *MT*, II .203.
10. Ibid.II. 203-5.
11. *AN*, III. 157-58.
12. *TA*, II. 470-71.
13. *MT*. II. 204.
14. As Beveridge, did, cf. *AN*, III. 157.
15. *MT*. II. 203-4.
16. Thus the *'Ibādat -Khānah* was originally open only to the exponents of Islam.
17. Vide, *MT*. II 175, in the year A.H. 981/1573-74 A.D.
18. Except for a few *Amirs* (nobles), all these categories represented the exponents of Islam, and this reference shows that the learned men of other religions were not yet admitted in the *'Ibādat -Khānah*.
19. Ibid, II.204-5. This has been corroborated by Nizamuddin *TA*, II. 428-29, 470-71, 514; and *Arif*, 40-41.
20. *MT*, II. 205.
21. Ibid, II. 205.
22. Cf. *Correia-Afonso*.
23. Ibid , p.53; and *B & L*, 117. Abul Fazl gives a different version of this episode, *AN* , III. 368-69.
24. Thus noted Abu'l Fazl: "The bigoted *'Ulema* and the routine lawyers (clerics), who reckoned themselves among the chiefs of philosophies and leaders of enlightenment found their position difficult. The veil was removed from the face of many of them" *AN*, III. 364-72 cf. *B & L*, 115.
25. *MT*,II. 211-15.
26. Ibid, II. 214.
27. *HMA*, II. 17.
28. *MT*, II. 262-63.
29. *AN*, III. 365.
30. *MT*. II. 263-64.
31. Ibid, II. 265-67.
32. Ibid, II. 268.
33. *HMA*, II. 20.
34. *AN*, III. 369-70.

35. *'Ain.* I. 164. cf. *B & L.* 132.
36. *Correia-Afonso.* 124-25.
37. *HMA,* II. 20
38. *Correia-Afonso.* 125.

Chapter-2

Situation of the 'Ibādat - Khānah

Badāonī noted: "On Friday after prayers, he (Akbar) would go from the new chapel (viz. the *Jāmi-Masjid* of Fatehpur Sikri which had been recently finished in A.H. 979/1571-72 A.D) of the Shaikh'ul-Islām (Salīm Chishtī) and hold a meeting in this building."[1] This reference has been largely misunderstood and misinterpreted. It shows the **sequence** of Akbar's movement, from the Jāmi' Masjid to the *'Ibādat - Khanah*, not the distance between the two buildings. Badaoni stated, categorically, that the *'Ibādat - Khānah* was built "**near the new palace in Fathpur**,"[2] which denoted the Imperial Palace complex situated within the *parkotā* (protective enclosing wall). He confirmed this in a later reference that the *'Ibādat - Khānah* was situated "**close to the Imperial Palace.**"[3]

Nizāmuddīn has not only confirmed the proximity of the *'Ibādat - Khānah* with the Imperial Palace, he has also added that it was founded "**by the side of the noble palace**"[4] which means that **it was built adjacent to the Palace.** As explained by his learned translator B.De.[5] the actual words of Nizāmuddīn are: "*dar-janah*" which mean '**by the side of**', i.e. adjacent to it. This reference pinpoints its situation more precisely than Badāonī's who uses the word *"nazdīk"* (near it).

These contemporary references show, unequivocally, that the *'Ibādat - Khānah* was sited within the Imperial Palace-complex, and within the *prakotā*-wall. Ignorance of these basic historical references, related to its situation, have led some archaeologists to trace its site near the *Bādshāhī-Darwāzah* (eastern gate) of the Jāmi' Masjid. outside the *parkotā* wall, far away from the Imperial Palace, at a common public place[6] where such an important Royal building could not have been sited.

Badāonī recorded an extremely significant fact in respect of the **situation** of the *'Ibādat - Khānah*. He noted:

> "He (Akbar) had the very cell *(hujrāh)* of Shaikh 'Abdullah Niyāzī Sirhindī (who had formerly been a disciple of Shaikh'ul Islām Chistī, viz; Salīm Chishtī, but had afterwards joined the circle of Mahādeva), **repaired, and rebuilt a spacious hall on all four sides of it.** He also finished the construction of the tank called *Anūp - Talāo*. He named that cell the *'Ibādat - Khānah*."[7]

This shows that the *'Ibādat - Khānah* was situated, not only adjacent to the Imperial Palace, within the *parkotā*, but also on the site of the *hujrāh* of 'Abdullah Niyāzī Sirhindī which was also, therefore, situated near the Imperial Palace, i.e. in the area which was later incorporated in the Imperial Palace. Literally, *'hujrāh'* denotes a cell, room or chamber but, here, it has been used with reference to the 'house' 'abode' or 'residence' of a Sūfī saint and here it denotes a **hermitage** or, more precisely, a *'khānqāh'* where he lived and also practised sufistic penances.

Owing to the **slope of the terrain** (viz. the Sīkrī ridge), the Palace-complex was laid out in several descending terraces[8] by filling the slopes and raising the edges to each **plinth level** evenly, and by building pillared *dālāns* on the face of each such filling. While the edge of the *Jāmi' Masjid* has a series of arcades below its eastern plinth (on both sides of the *Bādshāhī-Darwāzah*), pillared *dālāns* were built below the northern plinth of the *Mahal-i-Ilāhī* (so-called Birbal's Palace) **(Plate - 1),** the ridge sloping here from south to north. Double-storeyed *dālāns* had to be built on the northern side of the *Treasury* (i.e. below its northern plinth) (for section, see **Fig.1**) because of the larger magnitude of the slope **(Plates - 2-3).** Again, only single *dālāns* were built on the northern side of the *Ekastambha-Prāsāda* (the House of Unitary Pillar) and the court lying east of it, the slope being in a north-easterly direction **(Plates - 4 to 6).** These pillared *dālāns* (cloisters, verandahs) are there in-situ and confirm, without any doubt, that the **northern edge of the complex had been filled up and raised to its plinth level.**

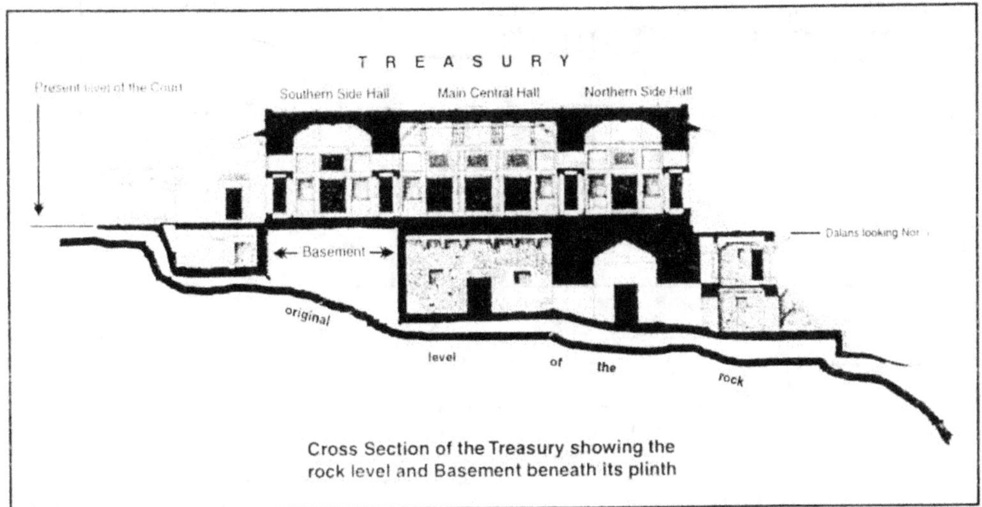

Cross Section of the Treasury showing the
rock level and Basement beneath its plinth

Fig.1

There is an open court *(chowk)* on the eastern side of the *Ekastambha Prāsāda* (west of the *Dīwān-i-'Ām*), on the north - eastern corner of this complex (Aerial Photo on **Plate – 7** and **Plates – 8-9**) (for site and plan, see **Fig.2**). It is situated on a lower level than the plinth of the *Ekastambha Prāsāda* (which is again on a lower level than the

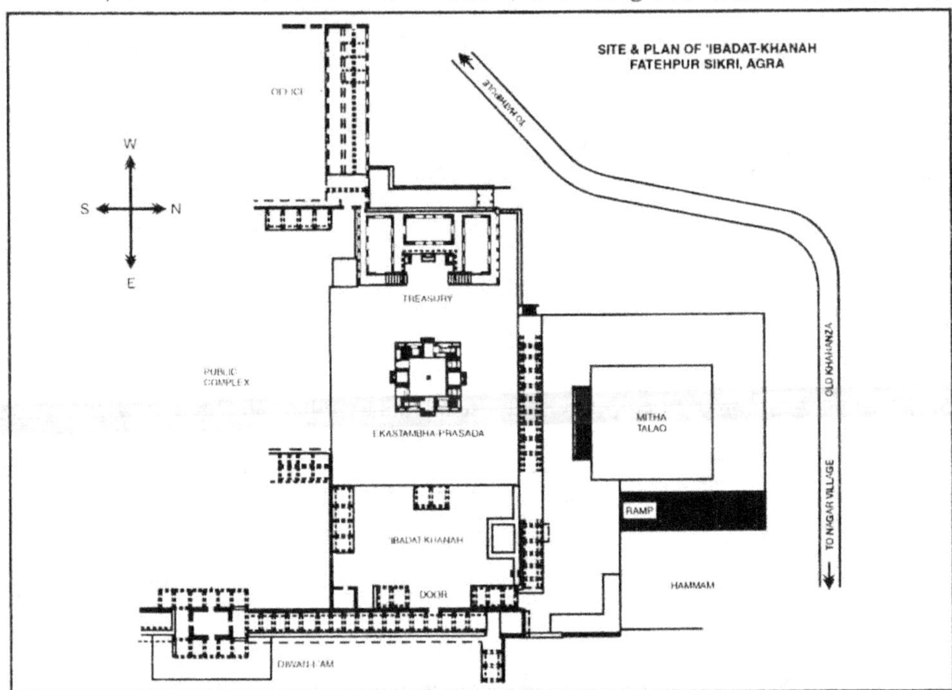

Fig.2

Treasury) (**Fig.3**). Though a historical building of singular importance, this court is lying **here unnoticed, unidentified and unnamed**. It must now be studied minutely with the help of contemporary histories, and the archaeological remains in–situ.

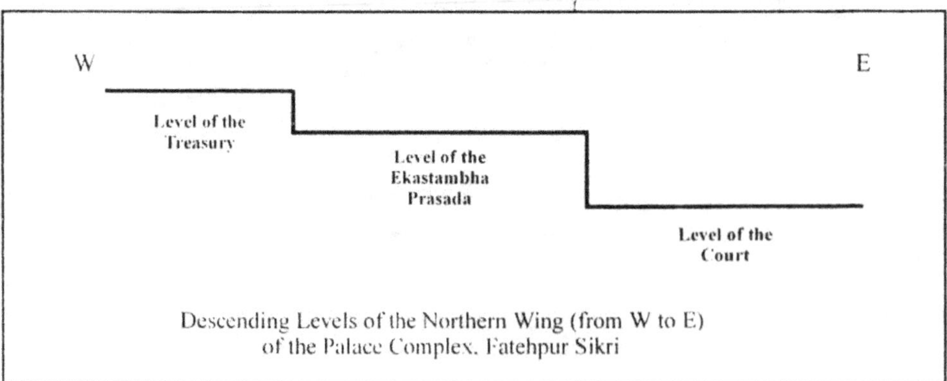

Fig.3

The stone pavement of this court bears a uniform design. On its three sides, East, South and West, are built pillared *dālāns (cloisters)* **(Fig.4) (Plates - 10-11)** which have covered (and disturbed) the pavemental design on the edges of the court, suggesting that they are later. There is a continuous *dālān*, situated **on a higher level** than the three *dālāns*

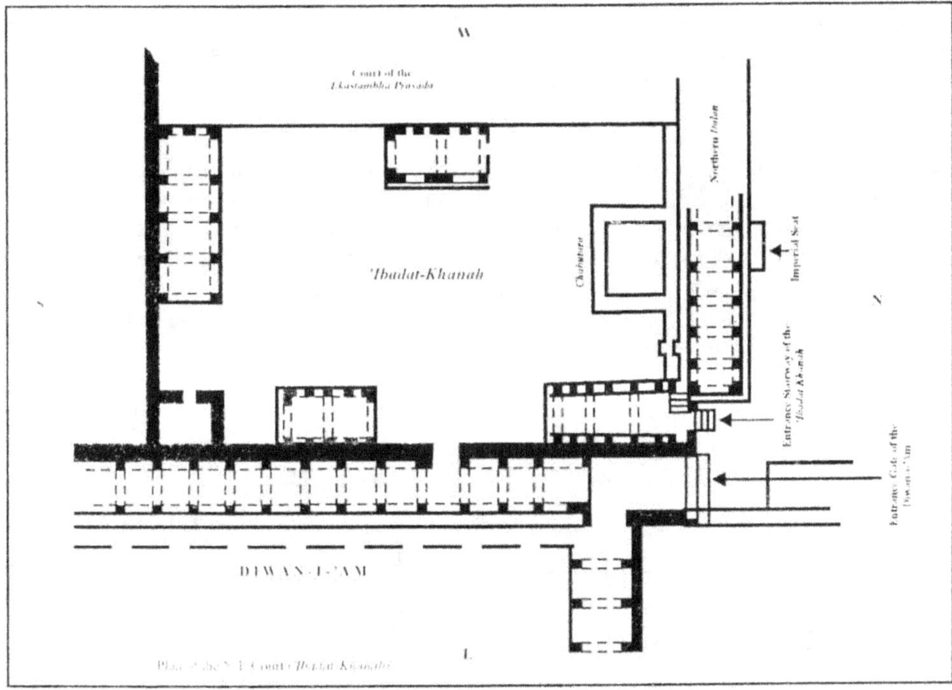

Fig.4

of the court, on the northern side **(Fig.5)**. It is extremely wide but it has a low ceiling **(Plates – 12-13)**. Except an extraordinarily large door-opening **(Plate - 14)** its northern side is closed, and it is open on the court side only. It is so detached and separated from the court, and is architecturally so placed as to preside over it.

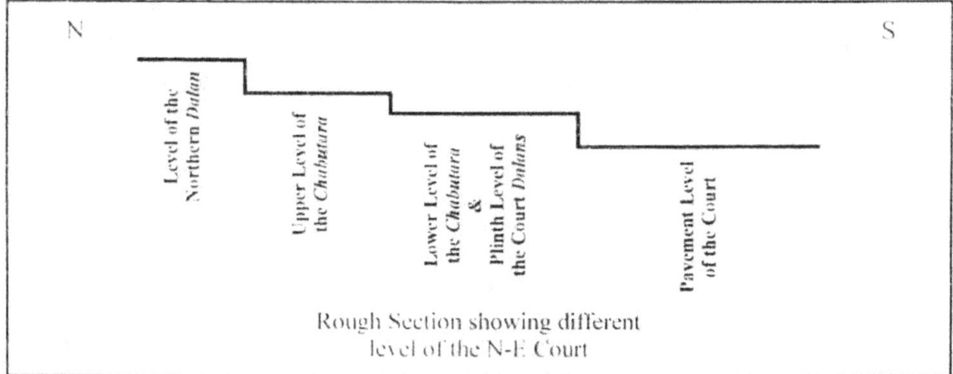

Fig.5

There is a two-tiered *chabūtarā* (platform) on the northern side of the court **(Plates – 15-16)** (see Fig.4). It is not attached to the northern *dālān* and there is a gap between the two, where some supporting stones have remained in-situ **(Plates- 17to19)**, suggesting that there was a *chhājan* (shade) on this '*antarāla*' (intermediary space). A pillar was originally there **(Plate - 20)** before the *chabūtarā* was casually repaired in the early eighties.[9] There should have been another pillar on the other side, supporting a wide *chhajjā*, which originally projected over the *chabūtarā*, bestowing an effect of prominence upon the northern section of the court, composed of the *chabūtarā*, the *chhajjā* and the northern *dālān*.

This is, in fact, the site of the '*hujrāh*' of 'Abdullah Niyāzī Sirhindī and **the site of the 'Ibādat - Khānah.** An old water tank of rubble masonry, with multiple staircases in-built on its sides, resembling an ancient '*kunda,*' was there on the edge of the rock near it, as inevitably needed by the side of a sūfī hermitage. This was also repaired and rebuilt with red sandstone by Akbar, along with the '*hujrāh*' of Sirhindi. The Palace Complex was laid out on one level and, therefore, the northern edge was filled up and raised to the floor level (of the southern edge). Because Sirhindī's '*hujrāh*' **was situated on the rock level, it was incorporated and concealed in the filling on the northern edge (Fig.6).** When the '*hujrāh*' was incorporated in the filling on the northern edge, a two-

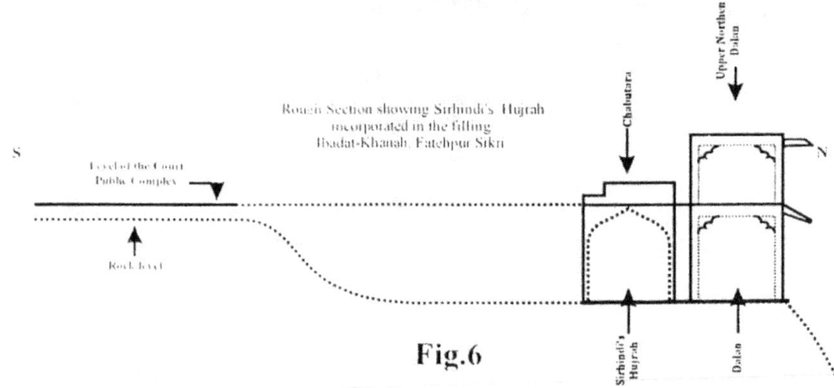

Fig.6

tiered *chabūtarā* was built on its vaulted ceiling. This was the usual covering of a vaulted or *ladāo-dār* ceiling built on the terrace, as is also there on the terrace of the adjoining *Ekastambha-Prāsāda*. *Dālāns* were built on all the four sides of the spacious open court. Badaoni's reference: "a spacious hall on all the four sides of it," [10] i.e. of the *hujrāh* of Sirhindī, can be understood only by this explanation.

This is the '*Ibādat - Khānah* (see Fig.4 and Plates- 9 to 12 above) which had, so far remained unnoticed and unidentified.[11]

****

References

1. *MT*, II. 204. This is confirmed by Abu'l Fazl, *AN*, III. 157; and Nizāmuddīn, *TA*, II. 470-71, who added that such meetings were also held on other holy and auspicious nights.
2. *MT*, II. 200.
3. Ibid, III. 163-64.
4. *TA*, II. 470.
5. Ibid, II. 470, ftn 1.
6. E.g. by *Rizvi*, p.43, *Gaur*, p 51 and *KKM, Appendices*, I. II. Their theories have been discussed, threadbare, and in full details, hereinafter in Chapter-5: 'Archaeological Analysis of the Recent Claims of its Identification'.
7. *MT*, II. 204.
8. *HMA*, II. 160, fig.40.
9. Loose pillar components of this site which remained there after this 'repair- work' were sent to the Lucknow Museum where they are preserved!
10. *MT*, II. 204.
11. Its present remains shall be studied in full details hereinafter, in Chapter-4.

Chapter-3

Composition of the 'Ibādat - Khānah

That the *'Ibādat - Khānah* was composed of four spacious halls (or *dālāns*) on the four sides is overwhelmingly supported by several other references of Badāonī and other contemporary eye-witness historians. Thus, Badāoni observed that the *'Ibādat - Khānah* consisted of four *'aiwān'* which his translator W.H.Lowe translated as four **'halls'.**[1] Abū'l Fazl confirmed that it had four *'aiwān'* which his translator H.Beveridge translated as **'verandahs'.**[2] Nizāmuddīn also recorded that it had four *'aiwān'* which his translator B.De translated as **'corridors.'**[3] De commented in the accompanying footnote that the proper term for *'aiwān'* would be 'corridor' or 'cloister'.[4]

The dictionary meaning of *'aiwān'* is a *sofa, portico, open gallery, verandah* (i.e. *dālān), balcony* (on the top of the house, for the benefit of the prospect and fresh air) and *palace.*[5] In fact, *'aiwān'* has been used as a general term for a hall or large room which is fully open. e.g. in the inscription of the *Khwābgāh* at Fatehpur Sikri;[6] and for large halls which are open on at least one side, and for that matter, for **portals**, e.g. in the inscription on the south portal of the main gateway of Akbar's Tomb Sikandara Agra.[7] But it has been used, more frequently, for *'dālān'* (cloister), e.g. by Badāoni in respect of the *dālāns* of the *Diwan-i-'Ām* of Lahore Fort;[8] and by Lahauri in respect of the *dālān* of Muthamman Burj Agra Fort[9] and the *dālān* of the *Dīwān-i-Khās* in the same fort (situated on its northern side, facing it, adjacent to the *hammām)*[10] and in numerous other references similarly.

In fact, there is no proper equivalent term for *'dālān'* (varandah or cloister) in Persian and the medieval historians have been using *'aiwān'* for *'dālān'*, as freely as for *'portal'.*[11] Distinction between them, and identification of either of them, can be made only by a close study of architectural remains in-situ. Thus, there cannot be four halls on the four sides of an open court, or a closed building, adequately separated, yet so interconnected as to allow **conferencing without confusion or intermixture**, and these references suggest, unequivocally, that the *'Ibādat - Khānah* consisted of an open court and four *dālāns* (cloisters) on its four sides.

Badāonī was constantly present in the *Ibādat - Khānah* with Akbar and he participated in its proceedings throughout, and his narrative is most reliable. He has left a useful record in respect of the four divisions of the *Ibādat - Khānah*:

> "Every thursday, he invited Sayyids, Shaikhs, 'Ulemā and Amīrs. But ill feeling arose in the company about the seats and order of precedence, so His Majesty ordered that the Amīrs should sit on the **east** side, the Sayyids on the **west**, the *Ulemā* on the **south** and the Shaikhs on the **north**. His Majesty would go from time to time to these various parties, and discuss philosophical subjects."[12]

Abu'l Fazl confirmed:
> "There were always four noble sections in that spiritual and temporal assemblage."[13]

and he also confirmed the seating arrangement recorded by Badāonī. Nizāmuddīn too confirmed the four sections of the *Ibādat - Khānah*[14], but differed in the seating arrangement which, however, is not a material point in this context. He also categorically mentioned that Akbar **"used to illuminate all the four assemblies** with his honour-conferring steps.[15]

Ārif Qandāharī, another contemporary historian, also gives some useful information. He noted that, in the courtyard of the palace complex, an (*'īwān-khānah' ='aiwan-khānah'*), was built which was *'chahar-khanah'* (**a four - sided building**) and had *'chahar-suffa'*[16] (four rows or *'qatārs'* of buildings). Whether these 'four rows' of buildings were on the four sides of a court or parallel to each other has not been mentioned by Ārif. There are no four buildings (halls or *dālāns*) parallel to each other at Fatehpur Sikri and, in any case, he meant, by this reference, **four buildings on four sides of a court**, as other contemporary historians have also recorded. Ārif's *'chahār-suffā'* has thus been used to denote four rows on the four sides of the court.

Badāonī and Abū'l Fazl categorically mentioned four *'aiwāns'* of the *'Ibādat - Khānah* and there is no other record by any other contemporary historian, of any other building which had four *'aiwāns'* except the *'Ibādat - Khānah*. It was only in respect of the *'Ibādat - Khānah* that four *'aiwāns'* have been specifically mentioned. Ārif Qandhari thus erred in a little measure, in naming this building (which had four *'aiwāns'* according to Badāonī and Abū'l Fazl) *'aiwān-khānah'* which plainly denoted a complex which had *'aiwāns'*, but he too meant nothing else.

Ārif's *'aiwān - khānah'* cannot be changed to *'īwan - khānah'* as Brand and Lowry did.[17] *'Aiwān'* is a hall open on at least one side; or a portal with a semi-soffit; or, more significantly a *'dālān'* (verandah), while *'īwān'* denotes the formal central portal on the facade of a mosque, tomb or any other building, and these two are two different terms.

'Īwān' cannot substitute 'aiwān' and, obviously Ārif Qandhari also meant **four 'aiwāns'** like Badaoni and others, when he described this building.

His reference to this building as 'chahār - khānah' has been translated by Brand and Lowry as "four-part house,"[18] which is wrong. It denoted a four-sided building with an open court in the centre, like the *catuhsālā* (four *sālās*, open pavilions, on four sides) plan of ancient Indian palace architecture. These translators have made arbitrary literal translation of technical architectural terms, and have confused the whole original Persian data.

It may be reiterated that Ārif Qandhārī's reference to 'chahār-suffā', denotes 'four rows' on the four sides of an open court, i.e. '*dālāns*' for which '*aiwān*' has been used. '*Suffā*' denotes the order and sequence of these '*aiwāns*' and it simply means four '*aiwāns*' (*dālāns*) on the four sides of the court, and there is no scope for any ambiguity.

All these contemporary historians, thus, confirm that Akbar's '*Ibādat - Khānah* at Fatehpur Sikri was a spacious building with a central *chowk* **(court)**, and *dālāns* **(cloisters,** verandahs) **on its four sides**, within the *parkotā* wall, large enough to accommodate 100-200 dignitaries who could sit there along with the Mughal Emperor, for the whole night comfortably, with Royal grandeur and security, and it was **entirely built of red sandstone**, like other buildings of Fatehpur Sikri.

The complex we have traced in the north - east corner of the Palace, east of the *Ekastambha-Prāsāda* and west of the *Dīwān-i-Ām* (Figs. 2 and 4 and Plates -7 to 12 above) fully responds to this description of the contemporary historians. These remains must now be studied in-situ, in full details.

****

References

1. *MT*, II. 200.
2. *AN*, III. 157.
3. *TA*, II. 470.
4. Ibid, II. 470, ftn.1.
5. F.Steingass, *A Comprehensive Persian-English Dictionary* (MM, New Delhi, 2000), p.134. Shireen Moosvi has translated it as 'porticoes' cf. *Episodes*, p.59.
6. Cf. *CAMA*, Persian text on p.51 and translation on p.40.
7. Cf. ibid, Persian text on p.52 and translation on p.41.
8. *MT*, II. 377.
9. *BNL*, I, II. 239.
10. Ibid, I, II. 238-39.
11. There is no equivalent terms of such *deshi* architectural terms as '*dālān*', '*jharokhā*' '*gaukh*' and '*chhatri*' in Persian and '*aiwān*' has been used for them. '*Riwaq*' is also used for '*portal*', as well as for '*dālān*'.
12. *MT*, II. 204-5.
13. *AN*, III. 159.
14. *TA*, II. 471.
15. Ibid, II. 471.
16. Cf. *B & L*, pp. 81-82: '*chahār - khāna*' '*chahār-suffā*' and '*ivān - khāna*' under the heading '*chahār - khāna*' '*chahār-suffā*' and '*General*'; p.108: '*chahār-suffā*' under the heading '*Ibādat - Khānah*'; and p.122: '*chahār - khāna*', '*chahār-suffā*' and '*ivān - khāna*' under the heading '*ivān-khāna*'. Tasneem Ahmed has not translated these portions and his reference to 'four rows' is as confusing as it is incomplete and deficient, cf. *Arif*, p.58.
17. *B & L*, p. 122.
18. Ibid, 122.

Chapter-4

Archaeological Study of the Remains of the 'Ibādat - Khānah

It has been alluded to above[1] that the court *(chowk)* located on the eastern side of the *Ekastambha - Prāsāda* (the House of the Unitary Pillar) is the site of the *'Ibādat - Khānah*. As the rock sloped from South to North, and also from West to East, it is situated on the lowest level (in the Palace Complex) three feet below the ground level of the *Ekastambha - Prāsāda*. It appears that the floor of this *chowk*, viz. the *'Ibādat - Khānah*, was paved when other buildings of the Palace Complex and the two tiered *chabūtarā* (platform) on its northern side (which covered the *Hujrah* of Shaikh 'Abdullah Niyāzī Sirhindī)[2] were built.

A continuous *dālān* (pillared cloister) was raised on the rock level, on the face of the northern side, **i.e. on its external side**; It is double-storied below the *Treasury* (Plates-2-3 above) (owing to the larger slope of the rock), and is **uniformly single-storyed** beneath the *Ekastambha Prāsāda* and the *'Ibādat - Khānah* (Plates - 4-5 and 6 above) on their northern side.

This *dālān* is composed of double square pillars, brackets and lintels, and flat ceilings. It is protected, on the external side, by a wide, slanting *chhājjā* which is also supported on brackets. Above the *chhājjā* is plain **frieze** which has arch shaped **holes** *(moris)* for draining out the rain water, suggesting that there originally was an open terrace upon these *dālāns*. Series of stone **hooks**, for tent ropes are embedded between the plain frieze and the cornice **(Plate - 21)**. It is noteworthy that such hooks were used ONLY and invariably, **at the edge of the terrace**, below the parapet *(mundair)*.

Above the cornice is the parapet on which arched merlons with lotus motif have been tastefully **carved** in stone, all along from one end to the other. This is the original construction and it shows, without any doubt, that there was no first floor *dālān* (above the northern external *dālān*) and the **curtain-wall**, made up of stone slabs, **now placed over it, is later**.

Only after a short interval, in the second phase of construction, *dālāns* were built on the three (east, south and west) sides of the *'Ibādat - Khānah* court, by which the design of the stone pavement of the court was disturbed testifying that **these court dālāns are later**. The ornamental border *(jhālar)* design of their plinths is also different from the original design of the main plinth, of the *Ekastambha – Prāsāda* court overlooking the *'Ibādat - Khānah* court, indicating that the two were not built contemporarily.

A *dālān* was also built on the northern side of the *'Ibādat - Khānah* court. Because the terrace of the northern (external) *dālān* was higher than the *'Ibādat - Khānah* court, the *dālān* which was built on it (the terrace) was also on a higher level than the *dālāns* of the court, and it was also **detached** from it. While square pillars, lintels and single bracket-stones were used on the court side to support the flat ceiling (of this *dālān*), short mini-pillars (viz. *gattū - khambhe*), lintels and similar bracket - stones were used on its external (northern) side **(Plates – 22-23)**. A **curtain wall** was placed on the parapet (*mundair*) (overlooking the northern side), entirely disturbing its function, testifying that former is later and the latter is earlier.

Series of narrow, oblong ventilators were opened in the wall that was raised on the curtain-wall. A flat *pattīdār* ceiling (in which plain stone slabs are placed across) was used on this *dālān* which was built all along the northern side of the *'Ibādat - Khānah* and the *Ekastambha-Prāsāda* continuously (Plates-13&15 above). This is a low ceiling, though the *dālān* is extremely wide; in fact, it is much wider than the three *dālāns* of the *'Ibādat - Khānah chowk*. Safe and secure, the northern *dālān* seems to have been **built for the exclusive use of the King**, just like the second story corridor of the *Panch - Mahal* and like that, it was also used by the King as the **Royal Corridor**.

Most interesting part of this building, however, is the **'Imperial Jharokhā'** which was built in the northern wall of this *dālān*, by cutting through the original parapet wall, overlooking the northern country–side **(Plates-24 to 27)**. With a width of 6 feet 3 inch, against its 6 feet height, **it is an extra-ordinarily wide opening**, the like of which is not there at Fatehpur Sikri, in the Agra Fort or in any other building of Akbar. It is unfortunate that it has survived in a much damaged condition. Out of its several ornamental door-jambs **(Plates – 28 to 30)**, one on both sides was either left unfinished or replaced in a later period. A wide *chhajjā* projects forward from its sill, at the even level, suggesting that there originally was a full *jharokhā*, closed by *jali* panels on the sides and a slanting *chhajjā* and superstructure over it. The brackets of the *chhajjā* have survived. Damaged projecting stones of the upper *chhajja*, bearing grooves have also survived. As a whole, it has been extremely tastefully composed in the form of a *'jharokhā'*; its **majestic size and form** testify, without any doubt, that it was a **'Shahi-(=Imperial) Jharokhā'** built for the **exclusive use of the King**. It faced the North and it should not be confused with the *'Jharokhā'* which was used for *'Jharokhā – Darshan'*, and which faced the East, the direction of the rising Sun.

There is not the least doubt that the northern *dālān* and the '*Imperial Jharokhā*' were built **contemporarily** with the *'Ibādat - Khānah* and are integrally related to its concept, as well as its **architecture**. The three were used **TOGETHER** by Akbar, at least from 1576 to 1582.

The *chabūtarā* situated on the northern side of the *'Ibādat - Khānah* court (Plates 12, 15,16, above) is two-tiered and measures as follows :

Lower terrace   31'-4" x 19'-5"
Upper terrace   21'-11" x 15'-1"

It is not connected with the northern *dalan* which is raised on a higher level. There originally was an '*antarāla*' (intermediary covered space) between the two structures. Its supporting stones which connected the two, have partially remained in-situ (Plates 15 to 19). There was a pillar on its western edge when this *chabūtarā* was restored between 1965 and 1972 (as shown in Plate-20). It was unfortunately uprooted and removed and lost to us and, to the building, during the so-called 'conservation'. There should have been another pillar on the other side, supporting a slanting *chhājjā*, more to give this section a **pre-dominant architectural effect**, than just to afford protection from nature. This *antarāla* too was built with the *'Ibādat - Khānah* and was integral to it (Plates 15 and 19).

The external (northern) *dālān* has an **offset** on its eastern end (see Fig.2 and 4 for plan) **(Plate – 31)**. The original entrance gate of the *Dīwān-i-Ām* was provided in this offset wall. It is vaulted **(Plate – 32)** and crooked. It has now been closed up. There is also an entrance door, 6' 8" in height and 3' 3" in width built on a considerable height **(Plate- 33)**. A stairway was originally used with it. It opened into the north-eastern corner of the *'Ibādat - Khānah* and descended on its north-eastern *dālān* by **four stairs**, rubble masonry skeleton whereof has remained in-situ **(Plate - 34)**. It was also closed up in 1965-72 and in our Plate 20 it is open. The stairs are 3 feet in width and 5' 5" in length.

This was the original entrance of the *'Ibādat - Khānah*. The gate given in the middle of eastern wall (measuring 7' 6" in width and 11' 9" in height) which at present gives entry in the court of the *'Ibādat - Khānah* **(Plates – 35-36)** is later[3] and, in all probability, there were **through dālāns** on the three East, South and West sides of this court.[4] The doorway was, in-fact, so planned and placed as to ensure only **selected and restricted entry** into the *'Ibādat - Khānah*.

This study of the remains in-situ leads to the inevitable conclusion that the northern *dālān*, with the *Shāhi-Jharokhā* and the two-tiered *chabūtarā* attached to it through the covered *antarāla*, was designed to preside over the *'Ibādat - Khānah* **complex** and, in all probability it was the **Seat of the King** when he conducted its proceedings.

The King's **security** was the primary concern of the builders of Fatehpur Sikri. Particularly, in the *'Ibādat - Khānah*, he **used to sit with** different types of people, of different temperament. Medieval intellectuals were, some times, vain and arrogant and Badaoni's narrative shows, illustratively, that at times, they fought with, and abused, each other! It must be noted that in the open court, the courtiers **stood** with bent head and eyes, and bound hands, and a court etiquette with strict discipline was enforced. But the situation in the *'Ibādat - Khānah* was quite different. **Here they sat** together, and at leisure, some times, for the whole night. King's security was the most important consideration in such a situation as this.

His personal body-guards were there with him. To reinforce his security, however, a **Guard-House** was built just on the first floor of the *Dīwan-i-Ām* entrance-gate, almost at the north-eastern corner of the *'Ibādat - Khānah* (Figs. 2 & 4 and **Plates - 37-38**). It is a square building of red sandstone (measuring 13' in length and 11' in width) which overlooks the *'Ibādat - Khānah* **reassuringly**. This Guard - house was also built with the *'Ibādat - Khānah* as its integral part.

It is noteworthy that a guard - house was, usually, built along with a palace used by the King (except his private palace) either for meeting his women (e.g. in the *Raniwās*, so called Jodhbāī's Palace) or his *chelās* (disciples) (e.g. in the *Mahal-i-Ilahi*, so called Birbal's Palace). It is indicative of the **King's presence** there. Here too, he met the intellectuals of the age. This guard - house testifies that this complex viz. the *'Ibādat - Khānah* was used by the King and **it was also an Imperial building**.

It must be pointed out that the **protective curtain-wall** of the northern *dālān*, on the external side was also **built to ensure security of the King when he was seated** in the *Shāhī-Jharokhā*. This guard - house is not related to the *Dīwān-i-Ām*, and it was not needed when the King was seated there because it had already been architecturally secured. The very situation of this guard - house on the first floor, adjacent to the *'Ibādat - Khānah*, shows that the **King used to be there**, and adequate arrangement for his **security** had to be made.

Outside this complex, on the northern side, are situated a large deep square tank, a full *hammām* and a *khurrā* (*kharanjā*, paved ramp) between them **(Plate- 39)**. The tank **(Plate- 40)** is built of rubble masonry and has intermittent stairways, on all sides, leading down to the water, just like an ancient *kunda*. It seems to have been built with red stone during Akbar's age. The *hammām* has the usual paraphernalia of halls, chambers, passages and tanks. It appears to have been sited here for the use of the participants of the *'Ibādat - Khānah*, which is why it was built just outside it (Fig.2). Its entrance hall has now been destroyed. It was also, thus, related to the institution of the *'Ibādat - Khānah*.

Akbar used to sit on the two-tiered *chabūtarā* along with *Badaoni*, Abū'l Fazl and other disputants, and also on such formal occasions when he received the Roman Catholic Padres from Goa. The Chester Beatty Library Dublin miniature (ms.3, fol.

263v)[5] **(Plate -41)** painted in 1604 by Narsingh for the *Akbar - Namāh,* in fact, **purports to depict this event of the 'Ibādat - Khānah**. It has been largely conceptualized, styled and stereo-typed. The King is the central figure of the painting and he is sitting on a *chabūtarā* attached to a building which has been **imagined** on the basis of what the painter had seen some 25 years before. It is important to note that the Mughal painter generally depicted the King in this style, in this particular 'right-hand' posture, sitting on a *chabūtarā* by the side of a building, as its central figure. He has been shown similarly, for example, in the *Akbar-Namāh* painting of the Freer Gallery of Art (No. 60.28)[6] **(Plate - 42)** and the *Akbar-Namāh* painting of the Victoria and Albert Museum London (Neg. No. S/9037).[7] This painting is ideational and imaginary but, fundamentally, it is related to this complex of the *'Ibādat - Khānah,* than any other building of Fatehpur Sikri.

It is in fact this *chabūtarā* which has been referred to by Abū'l Fazl as the '**lofty pulpit**' (mimbar)[8] and by Monserrate as '**high dais**'.[9]

Otherwise, and in the usual course, he sat in the northern *dālān* by the side of the *Imperial-Jharokhā* which was **his seat**. It opened towards the north which was deemed to be most auspicious and healthy direction. It opened on the country - side giving fresh air and afforded a vantage point to view the lake and natural scenes. The *Imperial-Jharokhā* too was integrally related to the *'Ibādat - Khānah,* in as much as the King sat here and watched its proceedings. It was also the seat of the King even when the *'Ibādat - Khānah* was not held and he was just relaxing and conversing with the special invitees.

It is very necessary to examine the **use, meaning and purpose** of this Imperial *Jharokhā* which measured 6 feet in height and 6 feet 3 inches in width. Badaoni has narrated some strange incidents that have not been explained so far. In his narrative of the year 986/1578-79, he recorded: "A Brahman, named Devi who was one of the interpreters of the Mahābhārata, was pulled up the wall of the castle sitting on a *chārpāi* till he arrived near a balcony, which the Emperor had made his bed chamber. Whilst thus suspended he instructed his Majesty in the secrets and legends of Hinduism, in the manner of worshiping idols, the fire, the sun and stars, and of revering the chief Gods of these unbelievers".[10] That his *'charpai'* was pulled up to the **balcony** and thus seated on it, and, **suspended in the air**, he instructed the King the principles of Hinduism, **was a novel and queer way of hearing**. One wonders why this *extraordinary* method of instruction was adopted. Devi could have been very well invited in his chamber and, seated comfortably, he could have instructed the King. This never happened before or after Akbar any where else, and this phenomenon is related to the mysterious personality of Akbar, several aspects of which have not yet been understood.

A sūfī saint Shaikh Tājuddin was similarly "**drawn up the wall of the castle in a blanket** and his Majesty listened the whole night."[11] He instructed the King in Sufism. Mulla Muhammad of Yazd, too "was **drawn up the castle wall** in the same way."[12] He instructed the King in Shia'ism. At least it is clear that all these three intellectuals who were pulled up the **balcony** were against the orthodox religion of Islam and Akbar heard them when they were practically suspended in the air, a little precariously, and it required extraordinary courage to speak against the established Canon Law of Islam to such a mighty ruler as Akbar the Great. Only **truth** could have saved them, and **it was this truth alone** which Akbar was trying to know.

All this happened at Fatehpur Sikri but the exact window, *jharokhā*, or balcony, situated on the first floor, against which each one was suspended has not so far been traced, simply because, careful attention has not been paid to this *Shahi-Jharokhā*, situated in this secluded corner, its architectural personality being almost entirely exhibited on the external (northern) side. Its width 6 feet 3 inch is extraordinary, and is almost equal to the length of a *charpai*. Devi was pulled up against this balcony and Tājuddin and Yazdi too were pulled up against it, and it is this *Imperial Jharokhā* which **was used by Akbar for this novel, albeit, queer experiment.**

Akbar used to sit here frequently, informally to watch the country - side; and also on formal occasions to preside over celebrations and other activities. **It was in fact, the Imperial Seat.** Abū'l Fazl narrated an event of 28 July 1582 when people assembled on the banks of a reservoir (tank) which was situated **"on the top of the hill of Fathpur, to the north of the dargāh,"**[13] and were engaged in Akbar's birthday celebrations. There is no tank situated to the north side of the '*dargāh*' of Shaikh Salim Chishti and Abu'l Fazl did not mean it. There is only this tank called '*Mīthā Talāo*' (Sweet Tank) situated on the top of the hill to the north of the Akbar's Palace-Complex which appears to have been referred to by Abū'l Fazl as '*dargāh*' (the House of Sanctity). There are overwhelming references in his *Akbar-Nāmah* in which he has invested Akbar with spiritual,[14] as well as temporal authority. He devoted a full '*Aīn* to this subject under the heading: 'His Majesty as the spiritual Guide of the People'.[15] Badaoni too noted that Akbar "called the face of the King, '*Ka'bah-i-Murādāt*' (sanctum of desires) and '*Qiblah-i-Hājāt*' (goal of necessities)."[16] In all probability, Abū'l Fazl referred to this Palace-Complex as '*dārgāh*' in the same hyperbolic zeal and he indicated this tank, viz. '*Mithā-Talāo*'.

The King was seated in the Imperial *Jharokhā* and the people came to pay respects to him. He was looking out on them when, all of a sudden, the tank burst. It caused some damage. Abū'l Fazl has described the whole incident and, in all likelihood, it happened here in front of the **Shāhī-Jharokhā** which was, beyond any shred of doubt, a place of singular importance related to Akbar's stay at Fatehpur Sikri from 1572 to 1585.

The archaeological remains in-situ, thus, testify that the '*Ibādat - Khānah* was originally composed of the following:

1.   a large stone-paved court (*chowk*);
2.   pillared cloisters (*dālāns*) on its three sides (east, south and west);
3.   a two-tiered platform *(chabūtarā)* on its northern side;
4.   a covered *antarāla* (intermediary space) between the platform and the northern *dālān*;

5. a wide *dālān* with a low ceiling on its northern side, situated on a higher level;
6. the *Shāhī-Jharokhā* which was used as the Imperial Seat;
7. a small doorway in its North-East corner (opening on the offset outside it) for restricted and selected entry;
8. a guard-house for the King's security;
9. a tank; and
10. a *hammām*.

With so many diverse components, the *'Ibādat - Khānah* was a large complex, of which only **fragments** have remained at present. How is it that, though it is situated within the Palace - Complex where the buildings have not been much damaged, it has been vandalized and demolished on such a large scale. This appears to have been done in the later, post - Akbar, ages **deliberately**. The Mullas and Maulvis were deadly against the institution of the *'Ibādat - Khānah* because Akbar used it to suppress the fanatic *'Ulemā* and to suppress the Islamic Orthodoxy. We know for certain that **Badaoni condemned it even contemporarily** almost to the point of abusing it:

> "which (the *'Ibādat - Khanah*) became by degrees *'Iyādat-Khānah* (the House of the Mentally sick)[17] and Mulla Sheri composed a *Qasidah* on the subject of which the following is a verse:
> 'In these days I have seen, united with the wealth of Qārun, the ritual of Phārun, and the Buildings of Shaddad' "[18]

This shows that the orthodox Mullas were biased against the *'Ibādat - Khānah* and they could let loose their anger upon its buildings, after Akbar's death. This explains why only its fragments have survived.

****

References

1.   In Chapter-2: 'Situation of the '*Ibādat - Khānah*'.
2.   This has also been explained above, in Chapter-2.
3.   It is too simple and rustic to be assigned to the classic age of Akbar.
4.   The *dāsā* slabs bearing the '*pān-pattā*' design can be inserted later, e.g. to replace the damaged ones, and this factor is not decisive of the original fabric.
5.   It was first reproduced in its *Catalogue* published in 1936. For its full reference, see Chapter-5 below.
6.   Cf. M.C.Beach: *The 'Imperial Image: Painting from the Mughal Court* (Washington D.C. 1981) Plate on p.119.
7.   Cf. *HMA*-II. Plate XIV.
8.   *AN*, III.365.
9.   Cf. Shireen Moosvi in *Episodes*, p.74.
10. *MT*, II. 265.
11. Ibid, II. 265.
12. Ibid, II. 267.
13. *AN*, III. 578-79. Beveridge's translation of *dārgāh* (*dār-gāh*) as 'gateway' is not correct.
14. '*Āin*, I. 166-67.
15. '*Āin*-77 of the First Book of the '*Āin-i-Akbari*, cf. ibid, I. 170-76.
16. *MT*, II. 266, 311 etc.
17. *Rizvi*, 43.
18. *MT*, II. 204.

Chapter-5

Archaeological Analysis of
Recent Claims of its Identification

There is a ruined, three-tiered, square *chabūtarā* (platform) lying haphazardly in a graveyard, at the corner made by the junction of the two roads: one from the *Bādshāhī-Darwāzah* (eastern gate) of the *Jāmī' Masjid* to the *Hāthī-Pol* (Elephant-Gate) of the Fatehpur Sikri township (south-north), and the other from this gate to the Palace - Complex (roughly, west-east), (Aerial Photos, **Plates 43 and 44**). It **was built of rubble masonry** in its original form **(Plates – 45 to 48** being photographs taken in 1984-85). It is situated, **alone and isolated**, in this secluded corner, without any walls, or **foundations** of any other building on or near it, except the boundary wall; without any **ceiling**; and without there being any other **building** attached or adjacent to it. At a distance of 39 feet 1 inch from it, on its south-western side, facing the north-eastern corner bastion of the Jāmi' Masjid, just on the road leading from the *Bādshāhī-Darwāzah* to the *Hāthī-Pol*, is a ruined arcade built upon the western boundary wall which runs from north to south **(Plate –49,** on the extreme left hand side). **Originally**, it was composed of two full plain arches and part of a central one, with *'Allāh'* inscribed on their spandrels in stucco, and **built entirely of rubble masonry.**[1] It has no ceiling, or any other building and it is, in fact, part of the western boundary wall of the **graveyard**. It is generally identified as a wall-mosque, *Qiblah-Wall* or *Qanātī-Masjid*, the like of which were built mostly in graveyards for such funereal rituals as reading of '*Fatihā*' (Chapter-1 of the *Quran* which is read for the peace of the departed soul, invoking God's mercy).

Its distance from the three - tiered platform, viz. 39'-1", is considerable (Plate-49 above) (**Fig.**7) and there is absolutely no doubt that it was not attached to the latter and, in fact, the **two structures were not related to each other functionally, architecturally or historically**. Had the two been connected, the wall would have been built adjacent to the platform, not at a distance of 39'-1" from it. **It is completely detached**. This is, in fact, a *Qiblah*-wall, denoting the direction of the *Ka'bah*, built to preside over the whole graveyard and to bestow upon it (i.e. the graveyard) a distinct religious character. Precisely, it was integrally related to the graveyard, lying east of it. This is obviously a later relic, as is the graveyard, and it cannot be placed in the age of Akbar.

W
Jami' Masjid
N-E Bastion
Road to
Hathi Pol
Distance 50 Feet
S
N
Boundary Wall of the Graveyard
Wall-Mosque (Qanati Masjid)
Distance 39 Feet
GRAVEYARD
GRAVEYARD
Platform
E
Distances between the Platform and the Wall-Mosque
and the N-E Bastion of the Jami' Masjid, Fatehpur Sikri

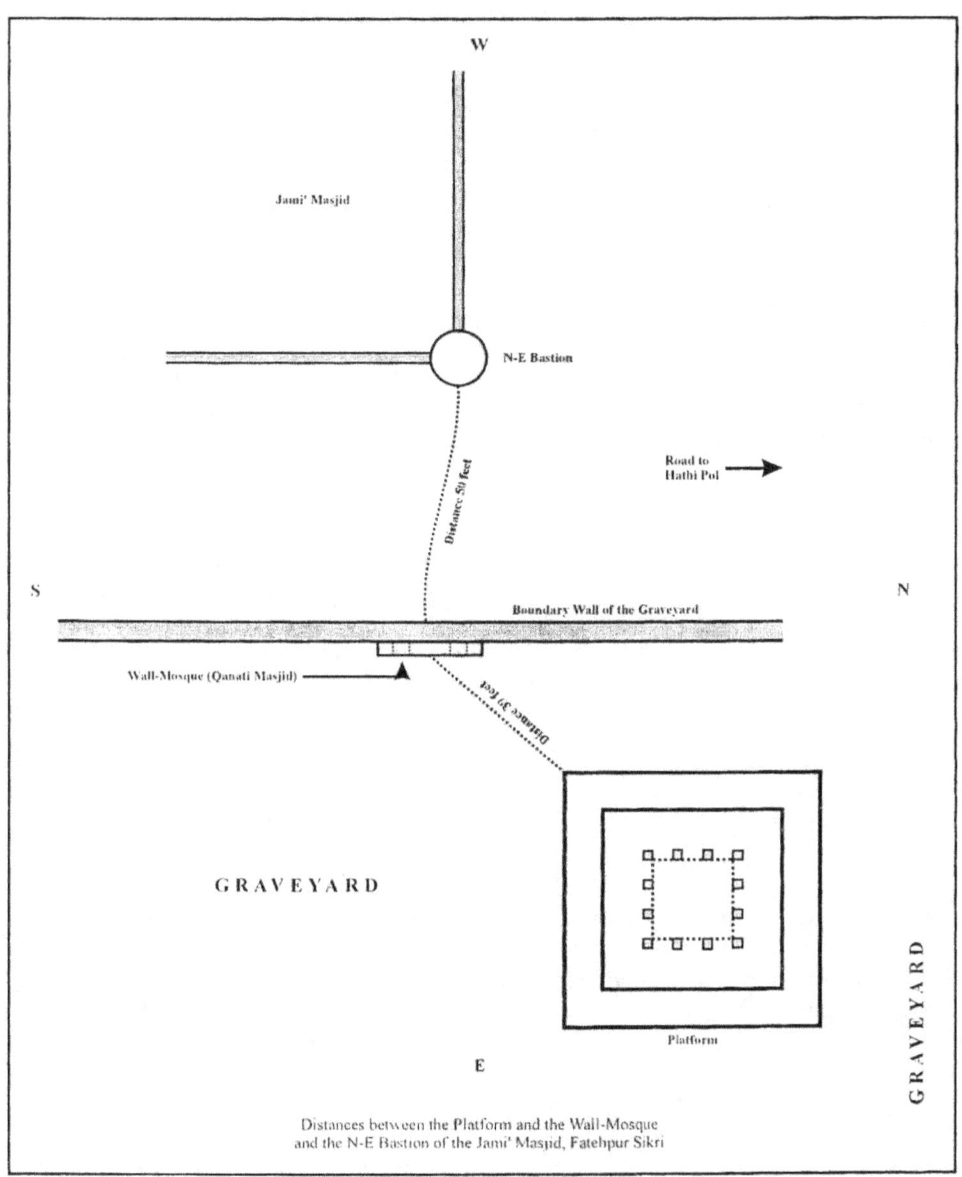

Fig.7

(1) Rizvi in 1972

S.A.A.Rizvi was the first scholar who identified this place as the site of Akbar's *'Ibādat Khānah*, on the occasion of a seminar held at Fatehpur Sikri on 2 December **1972**. His preliminary book, containing his discoveries at Fatehpur Sikri, was also released there in **1972**.[2] The square **platform was visible** on, and **above the ground even in 1972,** and no archaeological excavation was needed to reveal it. Thus he described the *'Ibādat Khānah* in 1972:

> "We believe that we have established its site with tolerable certainty.....Behind the principal *Haram Sarā* Palace (i.e. *The Raniwās*, so-called *Jodhbai's Palace*) and to the south of the high blank wall of the minor *Haram-Sarā* quarters (i.e. the *Shāhī-Bāzār* or the so-called Horses Stables), is a **tumbled mass of rubble, scattered with gravestones**, and scrubby trees. Every visitor sees it to his right as he walks up from the palace to the *Bādshāhi-Darwāzah* (the eastern gate of the Jāmi' Masjid), since the road passes quite close to a pillared red sandstone and rubble building still in fair preservation. The *'Ibādat Khānah* stands to the right of this: it is now a **MASSIVE RUBBLE PLATFORM, 19.50 metres** (=65 feet) **square**, covered with about 18 cms (7 inches) of lime mortar, visible at the edges, and appears to be piled high with a shapeless mass of **debris**; but on looking more closely one perceives the **outlines of a second platform quite clearly**. Heaped upon this is more rubbish, which might represent a **third platform**."[3]

This description of Rizvi testifies, without any doubt, that the platform could be seen and measured, and **all this was there, in 1972**, and there was no need for any excavation. The later claims that it was revealed in the eighties by excavation are all lies,[4] made for self-glorification.[5]

It is noteworthy that Rizvi did not find any **foundations**, or any other structure on or near it, and he also did not mention the ruined wall-mosque (*Qiblah*-wall) in this context, obviously, because it was not related to the platform. He noticed only a **three-tiered platform of rubble masonry** and he did not mention any brick or red stone work. As he was the first to reach the 'Everest', his observations are important.

(2) R.C. Gaur in 1978-88

It was at the initiative of Professor Nur'ul-Hasan[6] (Union Minister of Education, Former Professor and Head of the Department of History, Aligarh Muslim University), and to **answer specific question which he had in mind,**[7] that a National Project of Excavation was launched jointly by the Aligarh Muslim University and the Archaeological Survey of India, under the supervision of Prof. **R.C.Gaur** (of the

AMU) and W.H.Siddiqi (of the ASI). "The work continued for eleven years, from 1978 to 1988."[8] While Siddiqi has not published his report, R.C. Gaur's report has been published in 2000.[9] Gaur did not mention Rizvi and he did not acknowledge that Rizvi had already identified this site as the *'Ibādat - Khānah* in 1972, and had even measured it, though he was fully guided by Rizvi's findings.[10] Instead of being fair to Rizvi, Gaur himself claimed to have exposed the structure of the *'Ibādat - Khānah* in the years 1980-81, 1982-83 and 1983-84.[11]

Though he referred to the contemporary Persian histories of Badāonī, Abū'l Fazl and Nizāmuddīn,[12] he does not seem to have read them carefully and he missed the basic facts established by these histories, that:

1.   the *'Ibādat - Khānah* was situated **adjacent to the Palace-Complex**, within the *parkotā*;
2.   it had **four aiwāns** (*dālāns*) on the four sides of a central court;
3.   it was **spacious** enough to accommodate the King and 100-200 dignitaries for the whole night, comfortably and decently;
4.   it was a building which must have had a **ceiling** or ceilings, and **foundations** of walls; and
5.   **it was entirely built of red sandstone**.

Obviously, he was following Rizvi without finding any new evidence on the site, and without applying his own mind. This is more than illustrated by his claim to have found the house of Shaikh 'Abdullah Niyāzī; and "a few rooms which probably belonged to Niyāzī" in its neighbourhood,[13] **without an iota of evidence**, just to establish the *'Ibādat -Khānah* on this site. How did he identify the "unexposed house-remains of Shaikh 'Abdullah Niāyzī"[14] without any historical or archaeological evidence ? He just 'wished' it to be there, and it was there ! History cannot be reduced to a magician's art. It was all a pre-conceived exercise, and there is no substance in his claim.

Gaur erred in several other respects. What he called "its boundary wall 48 square metres, made of rubbles and bound by lime mortar"[15] was not the boundary wall of the platform, under study, but of the graveyard which came into existence much later,[16] suggesting that the boundary wall too was a later addition. What he called a 'mosque' (*Qibla-Masjid*)[17] was just a **free-standing wall** which was in no way related to the platform.

Gaur noted that this was "a pyramidal structure of three terraces built in diminishing order"[18] and that the first terrace measured 21.0 sq. meter, the second 13.35 and the third 6.70 sq. meter (**Fig.8**). According to Rizvi, the first terrace measured 19.50 sq. meter **in 1972**.[19] How it **expanded** to 21.0 sq.m. in 1980-81, as measured by Gaur, and who erred, is not known. The difference of 1.50m (equivalent to about five feet) is substantial and cannot be ignored. Gaur's measurements, however, show a proportionate one-third dimunition of the terraces of the platform.

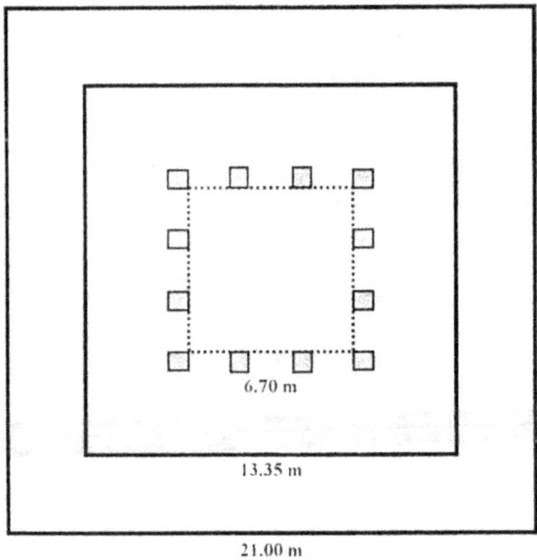

Measurements of the Three Terraces
of the so-called 'Ibadat-Khanah by Gaur (p. 52)

Fig.8

Gaur's observation that "the first terrace **might have** also been supported by a pillared verandah like the second terrace but no visible evidence is now available"[20] is a pure conjecture. Had there been pillars supporting a structure, **their bases embedded in foundations** should have remained in-situ, in any case, but no such foundations were found and he admitted that there was no visible evidence. Then how could he visualize a verandah - just because he **imagined** that it was there? He made an equally conjectural observation also in respect of the second terrace and imagined that '**perhaps**' it also "had a pillared verandah."[21] His observation: "The remains of the pillars and fallen brackets amply prove it" is too feeble to support his statement. Such **debris** do not prove the plan or form of a structure, without any foundations or pillar-bases embedded in the foundations. All these are fanciful surmises.

It is not known why Gaur did not measure the height of the first and the second terrace, and why did not he describe their composition, whether they were built of rubble or brick masonry and whether red sandstone was used on them. This was a National Project of Archaeology and it was expected that the Project directors would at least make a **faithful documentation** of the site, on which they worked, for the use of the posterity.

Most fantastic is his observation that there were two rooms on the third terrace "where the Emperor sat, **probably**, under a canopy" and one of the two rooms "was **perhaps** used by Akbar as his ante-chamber."[22] This is freak of his own imagination and is all false and misleading. As his own photographs, used in his book, show,[23] **stone-bases of pillars are embedded in foundations in the middle of the second terrace regularly.** Originally, there were twelve (12) pillars on all the four sides, supported on these square bases, four (4) on each side, making up a '*bārahdarī*' (with three openings on each side) **(Figs. 9 and 10** for conjectural restoration). A few have been destroyed **but four pillar-bases have remained in-situ on the western side** and three on the southern side, in this very order (see our Plate- 48 being photograph also taken in 1985).[24] Thus eight pillar-bases have survived (including the corner ones). The **stone slabs** of **the plinth** of the '*bārahdarī*' have also survived in-situ. **The crude and loose rubble masonry structure,**

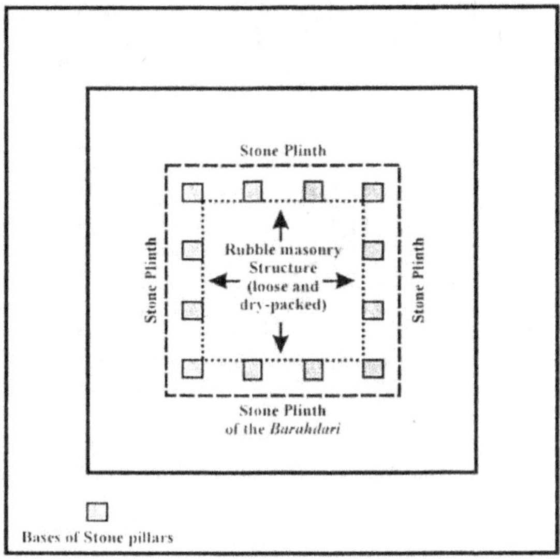

Plan showing Stone Remains
of the *Barahdari* in the middle of the Second Terrace

Fig.9

raised in the middle of the second terrace, between these pillars (our Plates –45 to 49)[25] is **a later addition** and it could not have been built along with these stone pillars and plinth; **the two are different architectural elements and cannot be inter-related.** While pillar bases and plinth stones are firmly embedded in the second terrace, this rubble masonry is **loose,** at places, **dry-packed** and it does not make any sense to assign this rough and rustic masonry work to the classical age of Akbar, unless one just wants to denigrate him. Gaur's observation of two rooms, anti-chamber and all paraphernalia[26] is not at all supported by archaeological evidence in-situ, and is pure fiction.

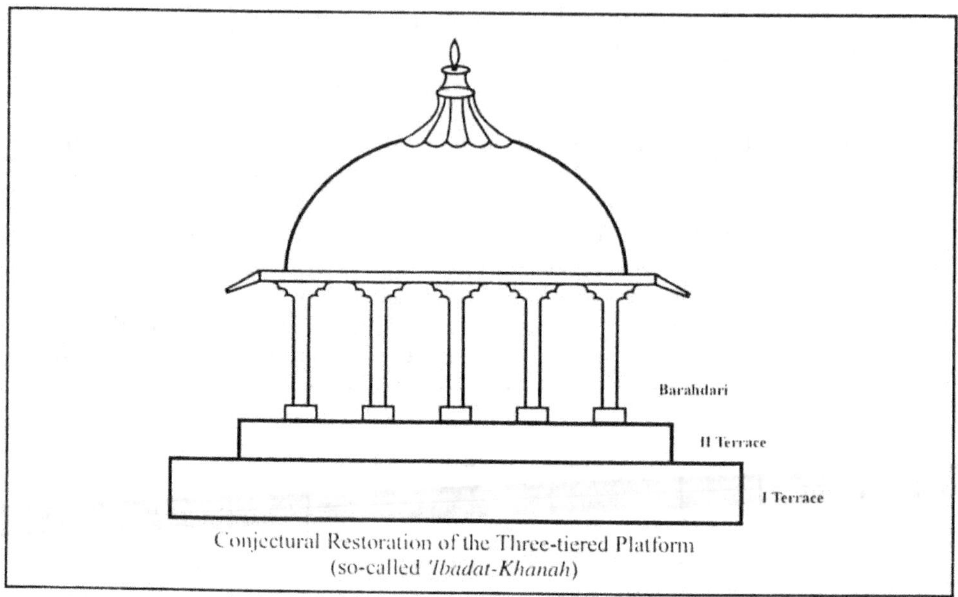

Conjectural Restoration of the Three-tiered Platform
(so-called *'Ibadat-Khanah*)

Fig.10

Therefore, there were **only two terraces** of this platform and a *'bārahdarī'* was there in the middle of the second terrace. The pillar-bases which supported this *'bārahdarī'* and its plinth stones have remained in-situ, as shown in **Fig.9** and Plates-45 to 49.

Gaur could not also explain how the four *aiwāns* (halls or *dālāns*), recorded unanimously by the contemporary Persian historians, can be accommodated on this platform, either on the first or the second terrace. This platform is a tiered structure and rises in elevation, **on the vertical axis**. The four *aiwāns* of Persian histories, on the other hand, extended on the plan, **on the horizontal axis**. It is architecturally not possible to fix up the latter in the former within such a space as this and, therefore, he preferred to ignore this point altogether.

Gaur referred to the *'Ibādat Khānah* painting[27] and noted that its details "more or less resembled with the structure revealed by our excavation."[28] This is patently wrong. As analysed hereinafter, the details of this painting **DID NOT resemble** this structure at all, and it was all a pre-conceived conclusion. Nor had he done any excavation on site and made any new discovery. **The structure existed above the ground in 1972**, as Rizvi's record, cited above, shows and Gaur's team just cleared it of vegetation and debris, **on the surface**. One wonders if 'surface clearance' can be termed 'archaeological excavation.'

But there is no doubt that this was done by his team under this National Project, between 1978 and 1988. Had any body else discovered it, he would have acknowledged it as he did in respect of the *Ibādat- Khānah* painting: "I am thankful to **K.K.Muhammad, one of our Technical Assistants** and an old student in the post-graduate classes for drawing my attention to this painting."[29]

It may thus be concluded, by a study of Gaur's so-called *Excavations at Fatehpur Sikri* that the platform was already there on the surface and Rizvi had already, in 1972, branded it *Ibādat-Khānah*, and **no excavation was needed to discover it**; and Gaur fixed up the *Ibādat-Khānah* on this site without ANY archaeological evidence, or any new material, purely on **surmises**. His interpretation was entirely subjective, which is why he could not advance this study from the stage Rizvi had left it in 1972.

(3) K.K.Muhammad in 2002

It is necessary, in this context, also to discuss here, the latest press statements of **K.K.Muhammad**, in the Daily *Jagran* Agra (Hindi) of 19 January 2002 (photocopy given herewith in *Appendix*-I) and the Daily *Jagran* Agra (Hindi) of 1 July 2002 (photocopy given herewith in *Appendix*-II). He claims that "symbols of several religions were there in the *Ibādat-Khānah* and there was a platform in its middle on which sat the followers of all religions and sects and made consultations."[30]

This is false and misleading. There were no symbols in the *Ibādat-Khānah* and there is no evidence, whatsoever, to support it. **It is pure gossip**. The contemporary Persian historians unanimously recorded that there were four *aiwāns* and the participants sat on the four sides, as has been discussed above. To say that they sat on a platform in the middle of the *Ibādat-Khānah* (which he reiterated in the later part of his statement),[31] is either total ignorance of the Persian histories, or **deliberate distortion** of the historical evidence: because only a tiered platform existed here, without any walls or foundations, he could have fixed up the *Ibādat-Khānah* upon it only in its middle, and it was all a subjective interpretation without any reference to historical or archaeological evidence.

As cited above, it was a National Project of Excavation, jointly undertaken by the ASI and the AMU, and the work continued from 1978 to 1988. K.K.Muhammad is **deliberately misleading** by suppressing this fact, and branding it just a Unesco Project on which, he says, excavation work continued from 1970 to 1982.[32] Is he fabricating a new chronology of this project and is **lying** just to fix himself in it, in an important position?

His statement that boy-and-girl students of the AMU did the excavation work under the direction of KK Muhammad and other professors, is also a **BLATANT LIE**. As noted above, the Project was jointly launched by the AMU and the ASI under the direction of R.C.Gaur and W.H.Siddiqi. **K.K. Muhammad was associated with it just as one of the technical assistants of the AMU**, as has been categorically noted by Gaur.[33] Instead of directing the Project, he was working under the direction of the Project Directors, viz. Gaur and Siddiqi, and **he was just an assistant**. But now, after an interval of two decades, he is trying to **plagiarize the credit** of the work done by his directors.

Some photographs used in Gaur's book may also be referred to in this connection. K.K. Muhammad is shown, standing alone amidst bushes, in Gaur's Plate XCVI, testifying that he was associated with this project (from 1978 to 1988).[34] Caption of Gaur's Plate-II reads:

"Professor A.M. Khusro, the Vice-Chancellor, AMU, Mrs. Khusro, Dr W.H. Siddiqi of the A.S.I. (both initially were Directors of Excavation)."[35]

But K.K.Muhammad is not there.

Again, caption of Gaur's Plate-III reads:

"The Member of the Excavation (A National Project) team from the AMU and the ASI. Professor R.C.Gaur, The Director of Excavation is also seen (4th from the right).[36]

But K.K.Muhammad is again not there. This shows that he was not occupying any directorial or supervisory, or any other important position in this project, and he was just one of several assistants working under the Project Directors. People may have short memories, as K.K.Muhammad believes, but photographs do not forget. These photos are betraying the **lie** which he is now propagating for self-glorification.

It is also absolutely false that it was **he** who revealed, by excavation, the remains of several buildings, including the *'Ibādat-Khānah*.[37] The so-called *'Ibādat-Khānah* platform was already there on the surface, in 1972, as has been discussed above; and his director R.C.Gaur was already studying it during the period from 1978 to 1988. If some **credit** of its discovery has to be awarded for **'surface clearance'** of this structure, it can be given only to the Directors of the Project, viz. R.C.Gaur and W.H.Siddiqi, and not to a technical assistant. Normally, several officials are associated with an archaeological excavation work, e.g. technical assistants, surveyors, draftsmen, photographers and foremen, and every one of them cannot claim to have discovered the site, as K.K.Muhammad is trying to do, after about two decades' interval. Whom does he want to impress by making such a **false claim of scholarship**?

His statement that Hindus, Muslims, Jainas, Parsees, Buddhists, Christians and **Sikhs (?)** sat (on the platform in the middle of the *'Ibādat- Khānah*) and **performed their respective worship and rituals on auspicious days,**[38] is altogether absurd, and betrays his total ignorance of the institution of the '*Ibādat-Khānah*.[39] It was not a temple, mosque, church or a place of worship, but a place of conference for discussions on religious and philosophical problems, and there is absolutely no record to show that any form of worship was held here. Perhaps, he has made this statement to project himself as a secular and liberal *musalman*!

In his subsequent press-statement in the *Jagran* of 1 July 2002,[40] K.K.Muhammad throws a challenge for a bout (*chunotī*), speaking arrogantly, like a village wrestler (*pahalwān*), that he was ready for it: "*bahas honi chāhiye, main to taiyār hun.*"[41] The only **evidence**, he cites over and over again, to prove his point, is a miniature painting which must, therefore, be examined in details.

Painted by Narsingh for the *Akbar-Nāmah* in 1604 A.D., it is entitled: '**Akbar presiding over discussions in the '*Ibādat-Khānah* '. The original painting is preserved in the Chester-Beatty Library Dublin (ms.3, fol.263v). It was first reproduced in the *Catalogue* of the Library.[42] Since Emmy Wellesz published it in 1952,[43] it has been widely published in almost all works on Akbar and Fatehpur Sikri,[44] and is known throughout the world for the last five decades.

K.K.Muhammad has not only **misinterpreted** it grossly, he has also **fabricated** the things which are not there in the painting (Plate 41). There is **only one terrace**, of low height, in this painting approached by a single stair and protected, on the edges, by a jalied balustrade. A carpet, with a uniform design, is spread on this terrace, from one end to the other. In the middle of this carpet, across it, is spread another carpet-*pattī* (long rug) on which two lamps and a *chowkī*, with some papers, are placed. One lamp is also there in front, just above the stair. Six courtiers (scholars) are sitting on this (i.e. the front) side of the *pattī*, two on the left and four on the right, with books. Outside the *qānāt* are shown two horses, two attendants, and a poor man, probably a beggar, with a child.

A small square carpet is spread on the distant side of the main carpet and Akbar is sitting on it by a large *masnad* (large pillow for reclining), under a canopy. He is facing the painting and he is its central figure. On his right are two courtiers (scholars), perhaps, Abu'l Fazl and Faizī, and two Christian Padres in their peculiar black dress. Two attendants and two boys, probably princes, are standing on his left hand side.

Behind Akbar is the corner of the *dālān* (verandah) of a *building*, and the slender pillar of the *dālān* is distinctly shown in the painting. Such **architectural parts of the dālān** as its **wall and roof** are also shown unmistakably.

A wall with four ornamental, semi-circular, cusped **arches, of uniform size and form**, and with an onion-shaped **dome** placed on its parapet, **is attached to the rear of** this building. A close and careful scrutiny of this painting itself, thus, testifies that:

1.   **There is only one terrace**, and there is no other terrace of this platform, in this painting. K.K.Muhammad is **misleading** by citing three terraces of this platform.

2.   **Akbar is not sitting in its middle but on its edge.** The personnel of the painting are occupying the whole carpet area. K.K.Muhammad is again lying that Akbar and the participants are sitting in its middle.

3.   **This platform is attached to a building** and, in fact, it extends forward from its *dālān*, on the front side. K.K.Muhammad is deliberately suppressing this fact and is **fabricating** a multi-tiered platform in this painting.

4.   The wall, with four arches of uniform size and form, is **attached** to the rear of this building. This is NOT a *Qiblah*-wall (wall-mosque) but the internal side of an enclosing (*parkota*) wall. It is a pity that K.K.Muhammad could not see **the building and its dalan** in the painting and he could not also notice that there was **no central Qiblah arch** in this wall, and it was just an enclosing wall, **attached** to the building. With a view to fix up the ʽIbādat-Khānah on this site, on the basis of this painting alone, he identified this wall (of the painting) with the *Qiblah-wall* or the *Qanātī Masjid* of the graveyard, discussed above, which **is situated at a distance of 39′-1″ from this platform**, and is not at all related to it (see Plate – 49). These are **two different structures**, of two different ages, but K.K.Muhammad identified **BOTH OF THEM** as the ʽIbādat-Khānah and rebuilt both of them anew, in the name of restoring Akbar's ʽIbādat-Khānah. **There cannot be a more outrageous archaeological exercise.**

5.   The four arches of the painting are semi-circular and cusped, and are uniform and of equal size. They are essentially **ornamental**, as is illustrated by the cusps of their intrados, vaulted semi-soffit and design of their lower part, all in stucco. There is no central *Qiblah* arch. They do not at all resemble the plain, pointed arches of the *Qiblah*-wall or *Qanātī-Masjid* which originally had a large central arch (viz. the *Qiblah*-arch), given in a frame which projected forward, and two smaller arches in each side wing (as shown in Fig.11). **The four arches of the painting are altogether different** and only a visually handicapped person can identify one set with the other. It is noteworthy that the arches, like those shown in this painting, were **NEVER BUILT** at Fatehpur Sikri, nor in any other building of Akbar, and they do not belong to his style of architecture.[45]

Fig.11

6.   The circular, onion-shaped dome shown on the parapet of this wall, in the
painting, is **imaginary and ideational**, as are the domes shown in the *Tutī-
Nāmah*[46] and the *Hamzā-Nāmah*[47] paintings. It was a **popular art-motif** of
Mughal painting. Such ornamental domes were shown on the superstructure
of buildings in Akbari paintings, as a matter of course, e.g.

   (1) in the painting from *Tarīkh-i-Khāndān-i-Timuriyyā*, c.1584 (Khuda
        Bakhsh Library Patna, No.107, fol.3b), cf. *Marg* p.106 Plate.7.9 (**Fig.12**)

Ornamental Dome, Painting from
Khandan-i-Timuriya, c. 1584,
Khudabakhsh Library Patna No. 107, fol. 3b,
cf. ibid, , p. 106, Pl. 7.9

Fig.12

(2) painting from *Harivamsa*, c.1585 (Freer Gallery of Art Washington, acc.No.54.6) cf. Ibid. p.104, Plate.7.7 (**Fig.13**)

Ornamental Dome, Painting from
Harivamsh, c. 1585,
Freer Gallery of Art, acc. No. 54.6,
cf. ibid, , p. 104, Pl. 7.7

Fig.13

(3) painting from *Akbarnama*, c.1590 (V & A Museum London No.IS-I-1896, 110/117) cf. ibid. p.17, Plate.1.1 (**Fig.14**)

Ornamental Dome, Akbarnamah Painting c. 1590,
V & A . Museum No. IS-I-1896 110/117
cf. Fatehpur Sikri, p. 17, Pl. 1.1

Fig.14

(4)   painting from *Changiznamah*, c.1596 (Worcester Art Museum, 1935.12) cf. ibid. p.110. Plate.7.13 **(Fig.15)**, and

Ornamental Dome, Painting from
Changiznamah c. 1596,
Worcestor Art Museum, No. 1935.12,
cf. ibid, p. 110, Pl. 7.13

Fig.15

(5)   painting from *Akbarnama*, c.1604 (Chester Beatty Library Dublin, ms.3, fol.263v) cf. ibid, p.32, Plate .2.5 **(Fig.16)**.

Ornamental Dome, Akbarnamah Painting c. 1604,
Chester Beatty Library ms. 3, fol. 263 v,
cf. ibid, p. 32, Pl. 2.5

Fig.16

This dome, in each case, is placed in the centre of the flat terrace like an upturned 'kalasa' or pitcher **ornamentally**, and it does not cover or roof the building on which it is used. It is not realistic and it also does not belong to the architectural style of Akbar, and there is not even a single example of such a dome in Akbar's buildings at Fatehpur Sikri, or anywhere else. It does not resemble, at all, the pillared *chhatri* of the North-East bastion of the *Jami' masjid*, which is composed of plinth, pillars, brackets-and-lintel openings, *chhājjā*, drum and cupola. Its **pillared composition** is distinctly visible and, by no stretch of imagination can it be compared with the onion-shaped plain ornamental dome of the painting (Fig.17). It is a mockery of common sense that K.K.Muhammad is identifying this dome with the pillared *chhatrī* of the North-East bastion of the *Jāmi' Masjid*, which is seen in its background, the *Qiblah*-wall being at a distance of 39′ 1″ feet from the platform (Plate-49), and the North-East bastion at a distance of 50′ feet from the *Qiblah* wall **(Plate - 50). The two are altogether different and make altogether different skyline.** It is a pity that though K.K.Muhammad has been working in the Archaeological Survey of India for quite some time, he has not yet learnt to distinguish between a '*dome*' and a '*pillared chhatrī*'.

As Plate-49 unmistakably shows, the cupola (of the *chhatri* of the N-E bastion of the Jami Masjid) CAN NOT superimpose the *Qiblah*-wall as shown in the painting; and it is not at all possible to see the *chabutara*, the *Qanati Masjid* and this cupola, TOGETHER, **in the alignment of this painting.**

This proves, beyond any shred of doubt, that the multi-tiered platform, and the ruined *Qiblah*-wall of the graveyard, situated at a distance of 39′ 1″ feet from it, cannot be identified as the building of the '*Ibādat-Khānah* shown in this painting.

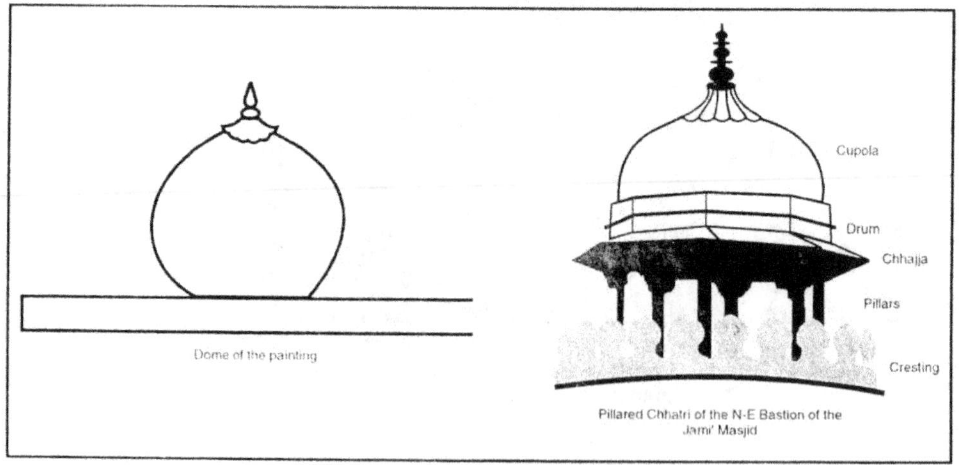

Fig.17

It must be clarified that the *Ibādat-Khānah* was completed in 1576, the Roman Catholic priests from Goa came to Fatehpur Sikri in 1579, and stayed there for three years till 1582. Thus, this painting is supposed to depict an event of the period from 1579 to 1582. But it was painted in 1604, long after Akbar had abandoned Fatehpur Sikri and it was practically a deserted place. Hence, **it cannot be a photographic representation** of the *Ibādat Khānah*. The artist composed it by memory and, like most Mughal paintings, it **is conceptualized and ideational**.[48]

The primary object of the Mughal painters was to show the King and the events over which he presided, e.g. court-scenes, hunting, celebrations etc; they rarely paid attention to the depiction of **architectural subjects**, which is how such major buildings of Fatehpur Sikri as the *Jāmī Masjid*, tomb of Salim Chishtī. *Buland Darwāzah, Raniwās* (so called Jodhbai's Palace), *Mahal-i-Ilahi* (so called Birbal's Palace), *Panch-Mahal, Khwābgāh,* the House of Unitary Pillar (*Ekastambha Prāsāda*), Dīwān-i-Am and *Dīwān-i-Khās* (so called *Daftar-Khānah*)[49] have not been represented in the paintings of Akbar's reign (1556-1605). This also happened during the reign of his son Jehangir (1605-27) when such a magnificant building as the tomb of I'timad-ud-Daulah Agra was not painted in his innumerous miniatures; and during the reign of his grandson Shah Jehan (1628-58) when the most beautiful and wonderful symbol of Mughal greatness, the **Taj Mahal** was not painted by the court artists, and not even a single painting of it has come down to us!!![50]

It must be borne in mind that Mughal painting was **never a photographic or realistic representation** of whatever architectural subjects it depicted. The Windsor *Bādshāh-Nāmah*, for example, has five paintings of the *Dīwān-i-Am* of Agra Fort,[51] but there is absolutely **no resemblance** with the real building which exists in-situ. Mughal painting was, essentially, **ideational and imaginary** and as such, the Chester Beatty Library painting cannot be deemed to depict Akbar's *Ibādat-Khānah* realistically, i.e. as it actually was, and it cannot be identified and 'rebuilt' in 'brick-and-mortar' on the basis of this single evidence.[52]

Besides committing these blunders of perception and judgement, K.K.Muhammad also ignored the following fundamental aspects of this matter:

7.   The platform (identified as *Ibādat-Khānah* by K.K.Muhammad) is **out of orientation**, i.e. its directions are not exactly East-West and North-South. This is an architectural '*vedha*' (or '*dosa*', fault or defect). This platform could not have been built in the age of Akbar (1556-1605) whose buildings face East or North **correctly**.

8.   Four '*aiwāns*' of the *Ibādat-Khānah* recorded by contemprorary historians unanimously, **CAN NOT BE ACCOMMODATED** on this platform.

9.   This platform is situated on a cross-road, in an odd corner, at a **common public place**, without *parkotā*, far away from the Palace-Complex. As reiterated by contemporary historians, Akbar's *'Ibādat-Khānah* was situated adjacent to the Palace Complex, and within the *parkotā*-wall, in accordance with the needs of the **King's security**.

10.   This platform is situated **in the vicinity of the toilets of the** *Raniwās* (so called *Jodhbai's* Palace), absolutely against the temperament (*mizāj*) and dignity (*shān*) of the Emperor Akbar, the *Shāhinshāh*, (the King of Kings) and *Zille-Allāh* (the Shadow of God on earth).

11.   It is **too small a place** to accommodate 100-200 dignitaries who could sit there along with the King, for the whole night, comfortably and decently, as has been recorded by contemporary historians.

12.   **No foundations** of any building, on or near it, have been found. The *'Ibādat-Khānah* was not held in a *'Shamiyānā'* (tent) and the record of the contemporary historians that it had four *aiwāns* testifies that it had a roof or roofs, supported on walls or series of pillars, foundations whereof should have remained in-situ in any case. Obviously, this is not the site of Akbar's *'Ibādat-Khānah*.

13.   It has also been made out by contemporary historians that Akbar's **'Ibādat-Khānah was entirely built of red sandstone**, like other Royal buildings of the Palace Complex of Fatehpur Sikri. But the original *Qiblah*-wall was built of **rubble-masonry** which was plastered over.   Red stone was not used on it. There were only two terraces of this platform and their **structure was also built of rubble-masonry** and, as it appears by the traces, stone slabs were used only on their edges. As discussed above in full details, there was a *'bārahdarī'* in the middle of the second terrace. Its pillar-bases and plinth have remained in-situ and they are of red sandstone. But even in its original form, it could not have answered the description of the contemporary historians.

His subsequent claims in this press-statement[53]   that **HE** found a mound on this site when **HE** came to excavate it, and it was the **GOLDEN MOMENT OF HIS LIFE**, because **HE WAS APPOINTED** owing to this discovery, are **all blatant lies**. It was neither a discovery, nor he discovered it. **He was only one of several technical assistants**[54] who worked there under the direction of R.C.Gaur and W.H.Siddiqi, as has been discussed above. He was occupying a subordinate position in this Project and he was not required to submit its report.[55]

Not only did he claim, academically, to have discovered Akbar's *'Ibādat-Khānah,* he has also **rebuilt,** anew, both the *Qiblah*-wall and the platform, in the name of archaeological conservation and restoration, in his capacity as the incumbent Superintending Archaeologist of Agra Circle of the A.S.I. He has rebuilt, at enormous cost, both the terraces of the platform (i.e. their floors) with red sandstone which was not there originally **(Plates - 51 to 54).** He has also extended the *Qiblah*-wall (*Qanātī-Masjid*) of the graveyard **(Plate- 55),** lying at a distance of 39'1″ feet from the platform, in order to bring it in line of the North-East bastion of the Jāmi Masjid, to prove its resemblance with the painting, and added three arches to it, a larger one in the middle and two smaller on the northern side. Their **form** has been changed and the broad intrados of the original two arches is missing in the three new arches. Instead of the **original material, viz. rubble masonry, the new arches have been built of Lakhauri bricks (Plates - 56-57,** showing the wall after the new additions were partially demolished on severe criticism in the press). Instead of the original cusped niche, he has built a plain oblong niche on the other side of central arch. Thus has he **altered the original form and fabric of these protected monuments, and he has destroyed their original historical character which is an offence.**

K.K.Muhammad has done all this for self-glorification: because Akbar's *'Ibādat-Khānah* had not been traced so far, and it was a hot controversy, he wanted to earn the credit of its discovery and, mounting upon the shoulders of Rizvi, Gaur and Siddiqi, he has proclaimed to the world that **HE** has found it and **HE** has restored it. He has not only squandered public money on this so-called restoration of the *'Ibādat-Khānah,* he has also committed an **academic fraud** upon the people of India.

****

References

1. Both these structures have been renovated and rebuilt recently (in 2002) in flagrant violation of the principles of conservation. The originality and historical character of these structures have been destroyed. The A.S.I. is not supposed to create new historical building. cf. *Indica*, 39.1. This matter has been discussed at length hereinafter.

2. *FPS* -72; his full book on Fatehpur Sikri was published later in 1975, cf. *Rizvi*.

3. *FPS* -72, pp 36-37

4. 'Excavation' involves **digging of the ground** through trenches. When vegetation, debris or any form of garbage is removed **from the surface of the ground**, to expose an archaeological site, it is not excavation but **'surface clearance'** which is technically called 'structural clearance'.

5. These claims of its identification have been discussed hereinafter.

6. *Gaur*, 73.

7. Ibid, Preface, p.vi.

8. Ibid, p.73 and Preface, p.vi.

9. cf. *Gaur*.

10. As a comparative study of *Rizvi* and *Gaur* amply shows.

11. *Gaur*, 50.

12. Ibid, 99.

13. Ibid, 50.

14. Ibid, Fig.8 on p.51.

15. Ibid, 50.

16. As *Rizvi* (p.44) observed: "when the enclosure began to be used as a **graveyard** is uncertain, in the absence of inscriptions on red **tombstones**; most likely when the disintegration of the '*Ibādat-Khānah* and the adjoining mosque was well advanced, perhaps **in the later seventeenth century**."

17. *Gaur*, 50.

18. Ibid, 50,52.

19. *FPS* - 72. p.37.

20. *Gaur*, 52.

21. Ibid, 52.

22. Ibid, 52.

23. Ibid, Plates. LXXXV to LXXXIX.

24. *A.S.I.* Neg. No. 2573-85.

25. *A.S.I.* Negatives No. 2326-84 and 2494-84.

26. *Gaur*, 52.

27. Ibid, pp. 50-52.

28. Ibid, 50.

29. Ibid, p.99, ref.No. 7 of chapter-14.

30. *Appendix-1*.

31. Ibid.

32. Ibid.

33. *Gaur*, p.99 ref. No 7 of chapter-14. This is confirmed by W.H.Siddiqi.

34. *Gaur*, Plate.XCVI.

35. *Gaur*, Plate.II.

36. Ibid, Plate.III.

37. *Appendix*-I.

38. Ibid.

39. It has been discussed above in chapter-1.

40. *Appendix*-II.

41. Ibid: that an officer of the ASI, a Central Government Department, could speak so wildly, without grace or decency, is unprecedented.

42. *The Library of A-Chester Beatty: A Catalogue of the Indian Miniatures* (ed. T.W.Arnold and J.V.S. Wilkinson) Vol. II (London 1936), Plate-36.

43. Cf. *Religious Thought as reflected in Akbar's Painting* (London, 1952), Plate. 33.

44. E.g. in *Fatehpur Sikri* (ed. By M.Brand & G.D.Lowry) (Marg Bombay 1987) Plate.2.5 on p.32.

45. *Indica*, 39-1, p.51.

46. Ibid, p.51 ftn.3.

47. Ibid, p.53 ftn.4.

48. Ibid, p.53.

49. For a study of these buildings, reference may be made to R.Nath, '*History of Mughal Architecture* Vol.II (New Delhi 1985); *Architecture of Fatehpur Sikri* (Jaipur 1988); and *Fatehpur Sikri and its Monuments* (Agra 2000).

50. *Indica*, op. cit. 53-54.

51. Nos. 10, 14, 19, 32 and 43, cf. *Indica*, op.cit, p.54. Architectural subjects have been depicted on a much larger scale in the paintings of Shah Jehan than in earlier ones.

52. Ibid, p.55.

53. *Appendix*-II.

54. *Gaur*, p.99, ref. No. 7 of chapter-14.

55. It must be noted that except for giving such wrong and misleading statements in the press, he has not been able to publish a paper in a research-journal, or a book on this subject.

K.K. Muhammad's Press Statement in the Daily Jagran (Hindi)
Agra - 19 January 2002

प्राचीन स्वरूप में लौटा 'इबादतखाना'

निज प्रतिनिधि, फतेहपुर सीकरी (आगरा)

संरक्षित स्मारक समूह में खंडहर हालत में मौजूद इबादत खाना अब अपने प्राचीन स्वरूप में लौट आया है। खंडहर हिस्से के अनुरूप ही दूसरे हिस्से को प्राचीन इमारत में मरकार ज्यों को त्यों बनाया गया है, तथा निर्माण को लेकर काफी भ्रम की स्थिति पैदा हो गयी थी। हिन्दू जागरण मंच के पदाधिकारियों ने नया निर्माण कराये जाने का अनेक शिकायतें दर्ज करायों तथा भारतीय पुरातत्व सर्वेक्षण के 22 माल रोड स्थित कार्यालय पर गत दिनों हिन्दू जागरण मंच के कार्यकर्ताओं ने भारी तोड़फोड़ करके विरोध दर्ज कराया है। इस तोड़फोड़ के पीछे असंतुष्ट पुरातत्व कर्मियों का हाथ होने का संदेह भी बताया जाना है।

उल्लेखनीय है कि दीवान-ए-खास स्थित दीन-ए-इलाही का स्वरूप तो केवल प्रतीकात्मक है। वास्तविक दीन-ए-इलाही का संदेश तो इसी इबादत खाना में प्रचारित किया जाना बताया गया है। उक्त इबादतखाना में अनेक धर्मों के प्रतीकात्मक चिह्न मौजूद थे। तथा बीच में एक प्लेटफार्म है जिस पर बैठकर सभी धर्मों के धर्मावलम्बी एवं मतमतांतरों के लोग आपस में मिल बैठकर सलाह मशविरा किया करते थे।

तीन दशक पूर्व यूनेस्को के सहयोग से फतेहपुर सीकरी में एक्सकेवेशन प्रोजेक्ट तैयार किया गया था। वर्ष 70 से 1982 तक अनेक स्थानों पर उत्खनन का काम चलाया गया था। अलीगढ़ मुस्लिम यूनिवर्सिटी के छात्र एवं छात्राओं ने के.के. मुहम्मद एवं अन्य प्रोफेसरों के निर्देशन में उत्खनन का काम किया था।

भारतीय पुरातत्व सर्वेक्षण आगरा परिमंडल के अधीक्षण मुहम्मद के.के. ने दो दशक पूर्व उत्खनन के दौरान ही इबादतखाना, इस्तखाना सहित अनेक भवन एवं इमारतों के अवशेष को बाहर निकाला था। उत्खनन के पश्चात से ही तमाम अवशेष यूं ही पड़े हुए थे। उत्खनन कर्ता के.के. मुहम्मद को गत माह अगस्त में आगरा सर्किल का अधीक्षण पुरातत्व विद नियुक्त कर दिया गया। श्री मुहम्मद अवशेषों को अब मूर्त रूप देने में लगे हुए हैं।

श्री मुहम्मद ने जागरण को बताया कि सीकरी के लोग बेवजह भ्रम की स्थिति बना रहे हैं अवशेषों को मूर्तरूप देना, स्मारकों की सुरक्षा एवं संरक्षण करना ही हमारा उत्तरदायित्व है। अनेक लोग न ही जानते हैं कि इसी इबादतखाना से दीन-ए-इलाही सर्वधर्म समभाव का प्रचार-प्रसार किया गया था। इबादत खाना के बीच म स्थित प्लेटफार्म पर हिन्दू, मुस्लिम, जैन, पारसी बौद्ध, क्रिश्चियन तथा सिख धर्म के लोग आपस में मिल बैठकर गहन समस्याओं पर विचार करते थे तथा अपने-अपने पर्वों पर विशेष पूजा-अर्चना करते थे।

संरक्षित स्मारक प्राचीन इबादतखाना नये रूप में। जागरण

K.K. Muhammad's Press Statement in the Daily Jagran (Hindi)
Agra - 1st July 2002

इबादतखाना पर बहस होनी चाहियेः मुहम्मद

निज प्रतिनिधि, फतेहपुर सीकरी

30 जून

लगभग दो दशक पूर्व उत्खनन में मिले इबादतखाना की प्रमाणिकता पर तूफान खड़ा हो गया है पूर्व अधीक्षण पुरातत्वविद् एवं कुछ इतिहास वेत्ताओं द्वारें इबादतखाना पर की जा रही टिप्पणियों से क्षुब्ध आगरा. सर्किल के अधीक्षण पुरातत्वविद् मुहम्मद के.के. ने कहा है सीकरी स्थित धार्मिक आस्थाओं के प्रतीक इबादतखाना पर अब प्रमाण सहित बहस होनी चाहिये तभी स्थिति स्पष्ट हो सकेगी। पर विरोधी बयानों एवं टिप्पणियों से 'इबादतखाना' पर धुधलका छा गया है। सीकरी में एक निजी समारोह में भाग लेने आये इबादतखाना के जनक एवं अधीक्षण पुरातत्वविद् श्री मुहम्मद ने 'जागरण' के साथ विशेष बातचीत चुनौती देते हुए कहा है कि अब समय आ गया है कि इबादतखाना की प्रमाणिकता सिद्ध करने के लिए बहस होनी चाहिये में तो तैयार हूं। मैंने खोज की है तथा पेंटिंग के आधार एवं अन्य साक्ष्यों से सिद्ध करूंगा कि इबादतखाना यही है। कैम्ब्रिज विश्वविद्यालय के स्कालर प्रोफेसर अल्सिन ने भी मेरी खोज को ही इबादतखाना माना है। अर्द्ध वृत्ताकार मुकीलों आंलकारिक मेहराब धार्मिक चिन्ह हैं। नम्बर एक बाउन्ड्रीवाल नम्बर दो प्लेटफार्म सीढ़ी नम्बर तीन प्लेटफार्म पर बैठे धार्मिक लोग, प्लेटफार्म चार पर पोशाक

सहित अबुल फज़ल और फैजी तथा फादर रुडोल्प फ्रोम इटली एवं स्पेन से आये फादर मोन सेरेंट काली ड्रेस में बैठा करते थे। प्लेटफार्म पांच पर शहशांह अकबर बैठते थे तथा नम्बर 6 दूसरे कक्ष का दरवाजा, नम्बर सात आर्च तथा नम्बर आठ सूफीसंत हजरत सलीम चिश्ती की दरगाह परिसर का डोम. दर्शाया गया है। इस प्रकार इबादतखाना के दुर्लभ चित्र को दर्शाया गया है।

उल्लेखनीय है कि फतेहपुर सीकरी स्मारक एवं इसके आस-पास वर्ष 80से 90

तक एक दशक उत्खनन कार्य यूनेस्को के सहयोग से चलाया गया था। उसी दौरान वर्ष 84 में इबादतखाना खोजना बताया गया है गत वर्ष तत्कालीन अधीक्षण पुरातत्वविद् धर्मवीर शर्मा ने वीर छबीलीटीले पर खुदाई करके जैन मूर्तियां निकाली थी। उस समय श्री शर्मा को कटु आलोचनायें होती रही। इतिहास वेत्ता डा. आर.नाथ एवं आगरा विश्वविद्यालय के पूर्व कुलपति डा. अगम प्रसाद माथुर ने बचाव की भूमिका अदा की थी किन्तु मामला 'अधकुचला' छोड़ दिया

उत्खनन में खोजा गया इबादतखाना।   जागरण

गया। यह कटु सत्य है कि फतेहपुरसीकरी अनेकों बार बसी है एवं उजड़ी है तथा इतिहासकार सीकरी के इतिहास से खिलवाड़ करते रहे हैं परस्पर विरोधी बयानों के बचाव एक मंच पर एकत्र होकर सीकरी के इतिहास एवं उत्खनन पर जोरदार बहस हो एवं स्थिति स्पष्ट होनी चाहिये। जिससे युवा पीढ़ी को दिशा मिली।

अधीक्षण पुरातत्वविद् ने बताया कि जब में उत्खनन के लिए आया था तो उस समय मुझे तो एक टीला मिला था जिसके ऊपर अनेक पेड़ खड़े थे दर्जनों पेड़ कटवाये गये धीरे-धीरे सफाई कार्य चलता रहा यहां तक कि हार्डबुश से भी सफाई की गई।

धीरे-धीरे कई प्लेटफार्म की परत निकलती गई यह टीला बादशाह गेट के उत्तरी कोने पर स्थित हैं। वर्ष 84 में सीकरी प्रोजेक्ट आर.सी. गौड़ के निर्देशन में तथा भारतीय पुरातत्व सर्वेक्षण के स्कालरों के साथ उत्खनन कार्य किया था। यह उत्खनन ही मेरे जीवन का सुनहरा पल रहा क्यों कि इसी खोज के कारण मुझे नियुक्ति मिली। पांच जून 1984 को अंग्रेजी दैनिक दी टाइम्स आफ इंडिया में प्रकाशित इबादतखाना खोज को पढ़कर तत्कालीन प्रधानमंत्री स्व. इंदिरा गांधी ने इसे महत्वपूर्ण 'डिस्कवरी' बताया था। पेंटिंग के आधार पर श्री मुहम्मद बताते हे कि उपलब्ध 'स्ट्रक्चर' को 1,2,3,4,5,6,7, तथा 8 नम्बरों से दर्शाया गया है।

1 : *Dalans* below the northern plinth (in the basement) of the *Mahal-i-Ilahi* (so-called Birbal's Palace) Fatehpur Sikri

2 & 3 : Double-storeyed *Dalans* on the northern side (basement) of the Treasury

4, 5 & 6 : *Dalans* on the northern side of the *Ekastambha Prasada* (the House of Unitary Pillar) and the Court lying east of it

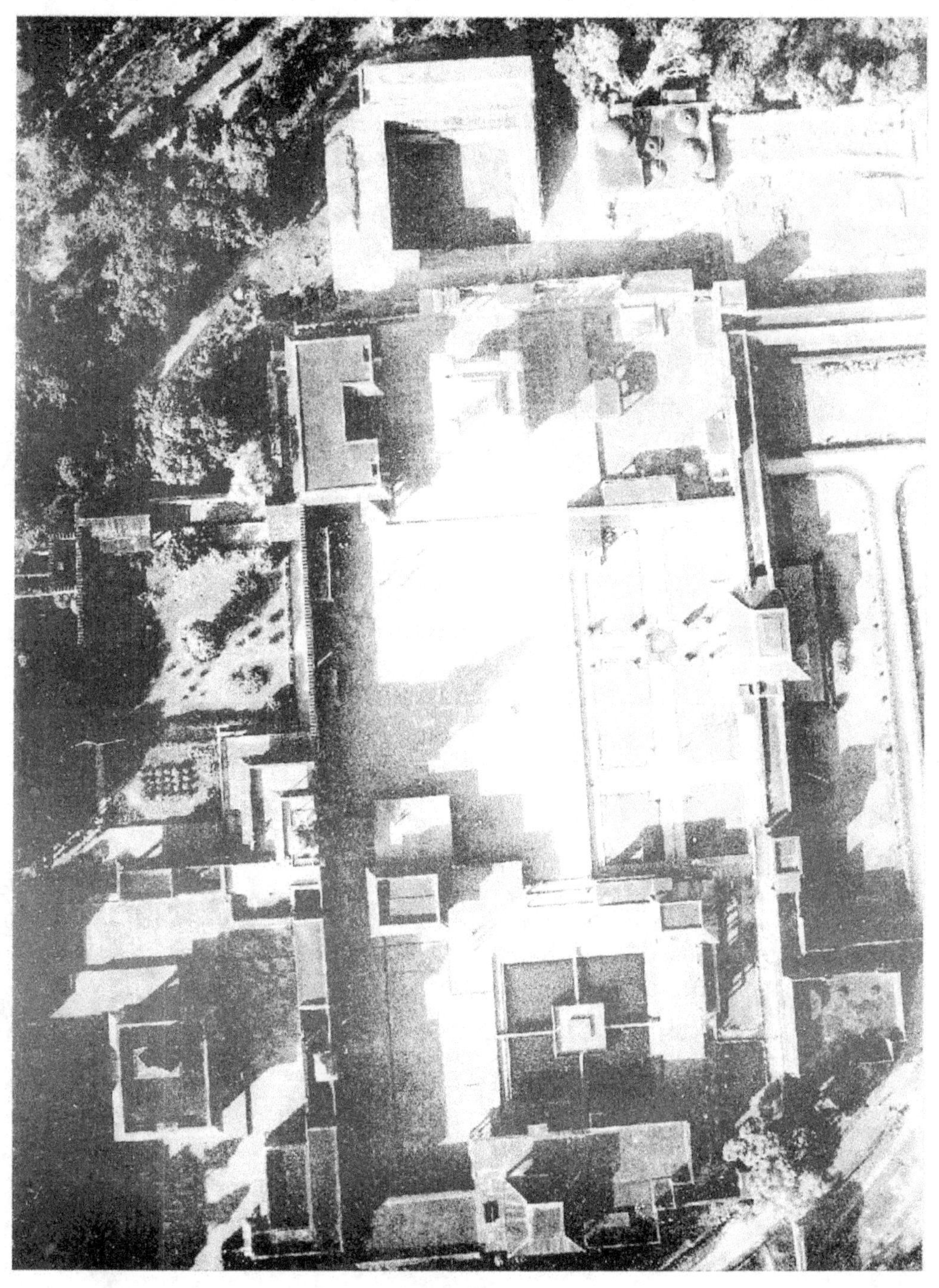

7 : Aerial Photo denoting situation of the *'Ibadat-Khanah* on the N-E corner
of the Palace Complex

8 & 9 : Situation of the *'Ibadat-Khanah*, east of the *Ekastambha Prasada*

10 & 11 : *'Ibadat-Khanah* : Court and the Design of its Pavement

12 : *'Ibadat-Khanah* : *Chabutara* and *Dalans*

13 : Northern *Dalan*

14 : Large Door opening in the Northern *Dalan*

15 & 16 : Two-tiered *Chabutara* on the northern side of the *'Ibadat-Khanah*

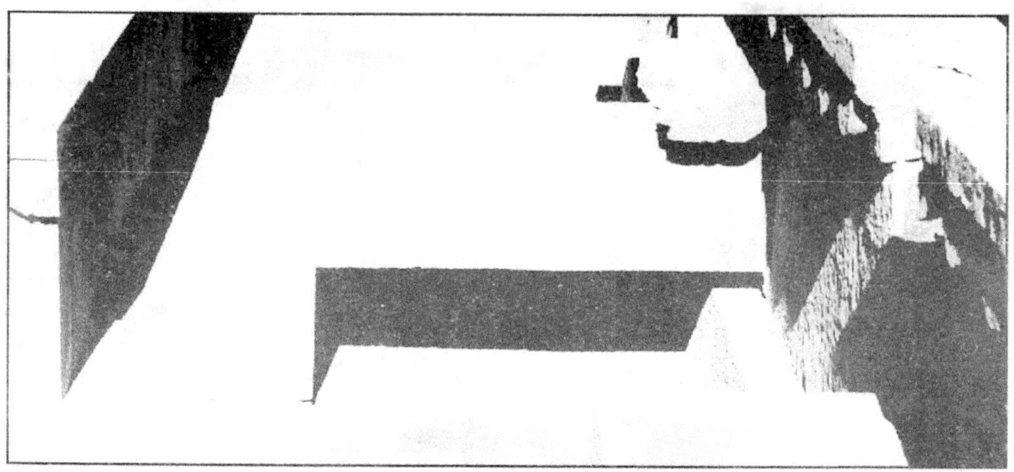

17, 18 & 19 : *Antarala* (Intermediary space) between the *Chabutara* and the northern *dalan* with remains of supporting stones

20 : View of the *'Ibadat-Khanah* in 1965 (ASI Neg. No. 1660/65) showing a Pillar of
the *Antarala* and the Entrance door

21 ; Northern Facade of the *'Ibadat-Khanah* showing the original *dalan*, *chhajja*,
frieze, parapet and the later curtain wall

22 & 23 : Mini-Pillars used on the external side of the Northern *Dalan* of the
'Ibadat-Khanah

24 & 25 : Imperial (*Shahi*) *Jharokha* opening on the northern side (of the northern *dalan*) of the *'Ibadat-Khanah*

26 & 27 : Imperial (*Shahi*) *Jharokha* opening on the northern side (of the northern *dalan*) of the '*Ibadat-Khanah*

13

28, 29 & 30 : Door-Jambs of the Imperial *Jharokha*

31 : Offset on the northern facade of the *'Ibadat-Khanah* (showing original entrance gate of the *Diwan-i-'Am* and entrance-door of the *'Ibadat-Khanah*)

32 : Closed Entrance Gate of the *Diwan-i-'Am*

33 : Closed Entrance Door of the *'Ibadat-Khanah*

34 : Internal side of the *Ibadat-Khanah* entrance door, with remains of the stairway

35 & 36 : Modern Entrance Gate of the *'Ibadat-Khanah*

37 & 38 : Guard House of the *'Ibadat-Khanah*

39 : Tank (*Mitha-Talao*), *Khurra* and *Hammam* on the northern side of the *'Ibadat-Khanah*

40 : The Tank (*Mitha-Talao*)

41 : The Chester Beatty Library Painting (ms.3, fol. 263v) depicting Akbar in
'Ibadat-Khanah, painted by Nar Singh in 1604 for the *Akbar-Namah*

42 : Freer Gallery of Art Painting (No. 60.28) of Akbar (from the *Akbar-Namah*)

43 & 44 : Aerial Photos showing situation of the *Chabutara* (platform) alleged to be *'Ibadat-Khanah*

45 : 1984 Photograph of the *Chabutara* (ASI Neg no. 2496/84)

46 : *1984 Photograph of the Chabutara* (ASI Neg no. 2327/84)

47 : 1984 Photograph of the *Chabutara* (ASI Neg no. 2494/84)

48 : 1985 Photograph of the *Chabutara* (ASI Neg no. 2573/85)

49 : 1984 Photograph of the *Chabutara* (ASI Neg no. 2326/84)

50 : *Backside of the Qiblah*-wall (of the Graveyard), N-E Bastion of the *Jami Masjid* and 50 feet space between them

51 & 52 : Newly Constructed (2002) *Chabutara* (Platform) alleged to be the
'Ibadat-Khanah

53 & 54 : Newly Constructed (2002) *Chabutara* (Platform) alleged to be the *'Ibadat-Khanah*

55 : Newly Constructed *Qiblah*-wall of the Graveyard

56 & 57 : The *Qiblah*-wall after new additions were partially demolished on severe criticism in the press